Hush Hush: An African American Family Breaks Their Silence on Sexuality & Sexual Abuse

A Collection of Personal Interviews

First printing 2007

ISBN 13: 978-0-9796619-0-7
ISBN 10: 0-9796619-0-0

Library of Congress Control Number: 2007929391

Cover art by Heightened Designs Unlimited, www.hducreative.com

Attention Corporations, Universities, Colleges and Professional Organizations: Quantity discounts are available on bulk purchases of this book for educational and gift purposes. For more information, please contact ILERA, LLC at www.ilera.com.

Hush Hush: An African American Family Breaks Their Silence on Sexuality & Sexual Abuse

A Collection of Personal Interviews

DeShannon Bowens

To the parents and guardians
who did not listen to their children,

To the families who needed help
and did not know how to ask,

To all those confused about
the true nature of their sexuality,

It's never too late to heal.

And to my cousin who lost his way,

May you find your true light on the other side.

Table of Contents

Acknowledgements

Sexuality and sexual abuse are still considered taboo subjects in the African American community. We have had an unfortunate history of having our stories told by other people, usually in a way that is inaccurate, demeaning or unfavorable. So first, I must thank the wonderful African American researchers, psychologists, sociologists, academic professionals and social activists who have made their work on sexuality and sexual abuse accessible. I'd also like to thank non-African American professionals and agencies who have made their research and statistical information available and easy to use.

People's stories are important. When someone gives you his or her story, you must care for it. If I did not have the trust of the Peterson family, this book would not exist. I am deeply humbled and grateful for the time they allowed me to spend in their lives.

There was invaluable support during the process of writing this book. I must thank Aquaila Barnes for her feedback and allowing me to showcase excerpts of this work at *Ascension's* monthly open mic night at the Harlem Tea Room in October 2006. I also must thank the actors who gave the Peterson family life that night by reading their testimonies. Thank you to Patrice Clayton for creating a warm and inspiring place. I spent many hours crafting this work over delicious sandwiches and teas at the Harlem Tea Room over the last two years.

Thank you to Stephanie and Mikel Alston-Nero. Your beautiful Stone Feather writers' retreat in upstate New York provided the peace, calm and tranquility I needed to have breakthroughs and overcome writing blocks while working through this material. Thank you so much for your deep enlightening conversation and friendship.

Louis Reyes Rivera's writer's workshop at My Sista's Place in Brooklyn, New York was a safe environment where I received constructive critique of this work. In addition, Louis' editorial services helped shaped this book and greatly improved my writing skills. Thanks Louis, the wisdom and guidance you offer as an elder gives hope and inspiration to up-and-coming writers.

When I needed her most, my best friend, Tiffany Green, stepped in to provide additional editing and feedback to make sure my work was sound and grammatically correct. Thanks Tiff, I don't know what life would be like without your friendship.

Praise and thanks to my powerful ancestors who always provide support and guidance. This book would not exist without the love, support and encouragement of my entire family, immediate and extended. Thank you Mom for always believing in me!

And most importantly, thank you to every survivor of sexual abuse who has shared your story with me over the last 10 years. Each one of you opened my eyes to problems I had not known existed. It is because of you that I figured out how I can be of service to others. Thank you for lighting the torch of purpose in me.

Preface

In America, we are suffering from a state of *dis-ease* that affects every person regardless of class, gender, age, spiritual/religious background, sexual orientation, ethnic group and race. The dis-ease I am referring to is the misunderstanding, repression and abuse of sexuality. There are state and federal laws to address our nation's illness as well as agencies with well-trained therapists, researchers and educators. There are documentaries and movies highlighting our problem in America. Fictional television shows have taken time to donate an episode or two to address our dilemma. Toll free 1-800 numbers exist to support survivors of this ailment, 24 hours a day and seven days a week. Yet, they are not the only ones who need healing and education. As a nation in a state of crisis, we all suffer from the same infection because we are all connected.

This predicament is worldwide, but for the purpose of this discussion, we are focusing on the United States of America. In our country, negative expressions of sexuality have resulted in: incestuous abuse, rape and the sexual molestation of children, teenagers, adults and senior citizens from all walks of life. Other harmful expressions lead to sexual harassment, sexism, human trafficking and violent pornography. People who are affected may suffer:

- Post Traumatic Stress Disorder;
- guilt from experiencing sexually abusive behavior;
- urges to inflict sexual abuse upon others after being initially violated;
- sexual identity confusion;
- depression;
- substance abuse;
- eating disorders;
- shame of their bodies;
- embarrassment from feeling sexual pleasure; and,
- an overall unbalanced, unhealthy perception of the self as a sexual being.

This illness has probably existed since human beings became aware of their power to impose control and dominance over another so, for once, we cannot simply blame our state and federal government. We can only look at ourselves and what we have been taught in this society about sexuality. Each of us must examine ourselves individually to consciously become aware of how we were programmed to think the thoughts that allow us to carry this dis-ease and spread it to others. After looking at ourselves, we must look out into our environment and identify the external and internal shaping factors supporting our present condition. All of the damaging manifestations of our sexuality started somewhere internally before they manifested externally.

There has been little work done that focuses on the *thoughts* and *beliefs* that affect the way we express our sexuality. In this work I explore the thoughts, opinions and beliefs of twelve adults within an extended family to better understand how we continue to disempower each other, generation after generation.

DeShannon Bowens

Spring 2007
Yonkers, NY

Introduction

I believe sexuality is sacred. When I use the word "sacred", I simply define it as, *something or someone worthy of respect*. The fourth edition of the *American Heritage Dictionary* also adds the word *venerable* to define sacred. The meaning of venerable is, *to command respect by virtue of age, dignity, character or position*. If we held up a mirror to American culture, many of us would see that our reflection, in the context of sexuality, is far from sacred. Popular and mainstream media has become saturated with images of misogyny and sexual objectification of women. News stories reveal that some of our entrusted religious leaders still continue to sexually abuse children. The number of sexual predators on the internet has not decreased since Chris Hansen's, *To Catch a Predator* series, which set up sting operations to catch potential child abusers, aired on Dateline NBC from 2004 to 2006. Once we shift our consciousness and view sexuality and each other as sacred, then and only then will we live and experience healthy sexuality in all aspects of our lives.

Sexuality consists of more than the act of having sex. Our verbal and non-verbal programming and conditioning play an important role in how we think, feel and express sexuality individually and collectively. Specific emotional incidents experienced in childhood can also shape how we connect to our individual sexuality on a physical level. For example, if someone constantly told a boy he was overweight during his childhood, he could develop a poor body image, which may affect how he perceives himself as a sexual being throughout adolescence and adulthood.

In my line of work, I am exposed to the suffering of individuals looking for answers to overcome and heal from America's rampant problem of child sexual abuse. Through my organization, ILERA Counseling and Education Services, I work with proactive agencies committed to educating their staff and client populations about cultural factors influencing and affecting sexuality. As a therapist, I have been blessed and honored to assist and serve people in a process of healing, discovery and empowerment after experiencing sexual abuse. This book is a contribution to educate and further guide the process of increasing our awareness about this problem.

Initially, I planned to interview African American women who identified as survivors of sexual assault. A few women agreed to be interviewed, but once it came time to talk about their sexual trauma and abuse history, they began to shy away. Soon after, I decided to write a book that would utilize research and statistical data to analyze child sexual abuse within the African American community. After composing a comprehensive outline, I realized I had overlooked the link between the prevalence of sexual abuse and how we are socialized to express and ironically, suppress our sexuality. My personal experience and education taught me that family interactions

2

provide some of our most powerful examples and models. Therefore, I changed my course once again and decided to let the stories of one extended African American family be the focal point of my book.

The first objective in choosing this format was to assess where we are getting our sexual messages from and how they infect and affect us. The second objective was to explore whether or not the messages and external cues we receive from others help perpetuate the silence surrounding child sexual abuse within families. For this reason, each family member was interviewed alone. This book does not present a detailed account of the history of sexual abuse and sexuality within the African American community from slavery until now. However, through the eyes of one extended family, it does provide a candid look at our present condition.

How I Met the Peterson Family

Once I decided to interview a family, I asked for volunteers and shortly afterwards individuals from an extended family responded to my request. I was fortunate enough to gain the confidence and trust of these individuals after explaining the purpose of the interviews and the reason I wanted to write a book on this topic. Some members declined to participate. Still, each person who agreed to be interviewed signed a release form granting consent to publish the results.

Interviews began in the winter of 2003 and ended in the summer of 2005. Speaking with the family members about sexuality made it more comfortable for them to talk about sexual abuse. The interviews became more personal as I asked "what if" questions and whether or not they knew if sexual abuse had occurred within their own family. I intentionally structured the interviews so that the questions about sexuality came before the questions about sexual abuse. It was easier for people to articulate opinions about sexuality in society versus the messages they learned from their own families. I was pleased that each person answered every question to the best of his/her ability, no matter how uncomfortable (s)he felt.

Who Are the Petersons?

The Peterson family is from Memphis, Tennessee. Within this family are four adult siblings (three sisters and a brother) who have their own immediate families. Mrs. Cole, Mrs. Walker, Mrs. Ryan and Mr. Peterson are all siblings. Their parents, Mama and Papa Peterson, are deceased. However, Mama Peterson was living at the time their interviews were conducted. The Peterson siblings all have their own children and some have grandchildren. I chose to interview only the adults, ages 21 and over, due to the nature of the topic. All parents and most of their adult children reside in Memphis.

Attention is given to the socio-economic status and education level of the Peterson family to show their diversity. (See Peterson Family

Tree and Bios.) Some Americans assume that a person with a high economic status and education level lowers the possibility of "bad things" happening within a family. We tend to think that the more "functional" a family *appears*, the less likely the children in the family will experience negative events. Dr. David Finkelhor and Dr. Emily Douglas, experts in child sexual abuse research, composed facts for the Crimes Against Children Research Center, which included research showing that children from lower income families are at a greater risk for sexual abuse.[1] However, the *source* from which any data has been gathered must be considered before making general assumptions or statements about a group or class of people. As a unit, the Peterson family demonstrates that other factors are at work. Unclear verbal communication, secrecy and personal opinion or beliefs based on inaccurate information can exist in any family regardless of their socioeconomic status. These factors can hold tremendous power and influence over how a child transitions through adolescence into adulthood.

The family I interviewed and many others so often wait for other people or institutions to tell us what our biggest problems are and how we should solve them. Currently, topics such as teenage pregnancy, sexual harassment, Internet sex predators, pedophilia and child sexual abuse are discussed publicly more than ever before. I was more interested, however, in identifying what parents say to their children.

In reality, the power of secrecy within a family is a difficult wall to break through. *Sexual Abuse in Nine North American Cultures*, contains a chapter co-authored by Veronica Abney and Dr. Ronnie Priest. They cite extensive research on the disclosure and underreporting of child sexual abuse in African American families.[2] Children's fear of being taken from their caretakers' home, the possible end of their parents or guardians relationship and shame are strong barriers. If families cannot communicate openly about sexuality, how comfortable will children, teenagers and adults be disclosing if and when they were sexually abused by someone in their families? As you will see in the following pages, whether the Peterson family knew it or not, all members have been influenced by American culture, African American family traditions and those peers closest to them, as it relates to their sexuality.

Peterson Family Tree and Bios

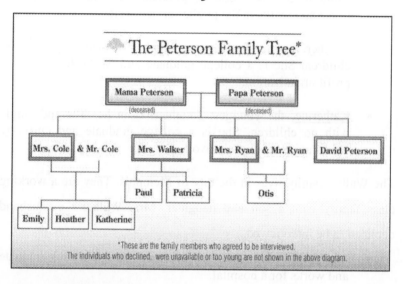

The Peterson Family Tree*

| Mama Peterson (deceased) | Papa Peterson (deceased) |

Mrs. Cole & Mr. Cole — Mrs. Walker — Mrs. Ryan & Mr. Ryan — David Peterson

Paul — Patricia — Otis

Emily — Heather — Katherine

*These are the family members who agreed to be interviewed. The individuals who declined, were unavailable or too young are not shown in the above diagram.

<u>Peterson Family Bios</u>**

The Coles are a middle class family living in the suburbs outside of Memphis. The Cole parents have been married over 40 years, and have three daughters.

- <u>Mrs. Cole</u> is in her 60s, a high school graduate and a retired business woman.

- <u>Mr. Cole</u> is in his 60s, a college graduate and recently retired from a career in hotel management.

** The names, geographical location and personal occupations of the family members have been changed in order to protect their identity. An equivalent occupation based on income level was substituted. However, their gender, age, familial relations, education level, socio-economic status and personal accounts are true.

- Emily, the oldest daughter, is in her 40s and divorced with no children. She is a college graduate, residing on the West Coast and works in the public service sector.

- Heather, the middle daughter, is in her 30s and single with no children. She is a college graduate and works for a not for profit organization.

- Katherine, the youngest daughter, is in her 30s and single with no children. She is a college graduate and currently works as a school social worker.

The Walker family lives in the city of Memphis. They are a working class family with a son and daughter. Mrs. Walker's ex-husband declined to be interviewed.

- Mrs. Walker is in her 50s, divorced, a high school graduate and works for a hospital.

- Paul, the oldest, is in his 30s. He is a high school graduate, self-employed, single and has two daughters.

- Patricia, the youngest, is in her 20s. She is a full-time undergraduate college student, single and has one son.

The Ryan family is also a working class family who lives in a suburb outside of Memphis. The Ryan parents are retired and have been married for more than 30 years. They have three sons. One son declined to participate in the interview and the other could not be reached.

- Mrs. Ryan is in her 60s, a high school graduate and retired from working as an office manager.

- Mr. Ryan is in his 60s, a high school graduate and retired from construction work.

- Otis, the oldest son, is in his 30s. He is a high school graduate, works at a restaurant and is married with a son and daughter.

Mr. David Peterson is in his 40s and the youngest of his siblings in the Peterson family. He is a high school graduate who lives with relatives in the city of Memphis. Currently, Mr. Peterson is unemployed and separated from his wife. They have three children, two daughters and a son. Due to their personal circumstances, I did not attempt to contact his wife.

Chapter 1

Sexuality Awareness

Our awareness as sexual beings begins by the time we are toddlers. It could be something as innocent as a child playing in a bathtub or a neighborhood friend sharing information (s)he received from an older peer or adult. The point is our awareness begins with observation and experience. Maybe it happens when a girl notices she has different body parts from a boy. Perhaps a child notices his/her parents or guardians kissing. One day, the same child may hear strange noises coming from Mommy and Daddy's bedroom, knock on the door and ask, "What ya doing in there?" Such incidents are innocent reflections of a curious child. Unfortunately, children and teenagers can have other experiences that are confusing, emotionally disturbing and traumatic.

Sexuality is a challenging topic for people to discuss. Sexual abuse is even more difficult. In an effort to stimulate thoughts on the subject of sexuality and keep resistance minimal, I asked a personal question that was broad enough to keep the Peterson family engaged. Since this was the first question, many of the family members' answers are brief. However, as we proceed further with the interviews, each member of the Peterson family opens up in his/her own unique way.

Meet the Coles

Mr. Cole, Mrs. Cole, Emily, Heather and Katherine all have distinct personalities. Everyone in this particular family appeared comfortable during their interviews. For Mrs. Cole's interview, we sat in her cozy office where she answered my questions. She smiled a lot and didn't appear the least bit perplexed until we got into questions focusing on the possibility of sexual abuse within her family. (See Chapter 7 for Mrs. Cole's response.)

During Mr. Cole's interview, we sat on the couch in the basement of their home. He had the television on but was kind enough to put the football game on mute while we talked. His demeanor was very relaxed and laid-back throughout the majority of the interview.

Emily, the oldest daughter, is by far the sassiest. I was fortunate enough to interview her in person while she was visiting her parents. We talked at great length in a spare bedroom of her parents' home. She was quite humorous and animated. Undoubtedly, Emily was one of the most forthcoming individuals in her immediate family and the Petersons as a whole.

Heather, the middle child, had her interview by phone. I was unable to fully discern her comfort level and demeanor since we were not speaking in person. She sounded tired but still answered all of my questions willingly.

Katherine, the youngest of the Cole children, was the first person interviewed in the Cole Family. I conducted her interview at her home. Similar to her father, she also had the TV on. Her disposition was friendly, and she gave extra consideration to the questions that specifically pertained to her.

Notice the different experiences of each member of the Cole Family as they answer the first question, *"Where did you receive your first messages about sexuality?"*

COLE FAMILY

<u>Mrs. Cole</u>
For me, it was friends and school. I had a health class when I was a junior in high school. Afterwards, my best friend and I would discuss the things we learned. Our reactions were, *"We never did anything like that [sex]. That doesn't sound right. It [sex] sounds gross!"*

At the time we were growing up, you didn't just walk around and talk about it. I didn't see a lot of it on TV, so I didn't have questions to ask. Someone who had a TV could probably inquire about sex and sexuality more.

<u>Mr. Cole</u>
In grade school, we received messages that girls were different from boys. We started flirting with them to show off.

13

Emily

At nine or ten, my earliest messages came from books. When my grandfather died, we went through his bookcase. I took the books I thought were interesting. The main one which caught my attention was a romance novel, *Sweet Savage Love*. After I read it, I passed it to my girlfriend. My friends and I would use our allowances to purchase books by that same author and many others. My parents figured out I was reading them three to four years later and had a cow!

Prior to books, I had a knowledge of what stuff [sex] was. Around age seven, I asked my mother questions like, *"Mommy, what's that? Why don't they [boys] have what we have?"* But I'm certain my first real reference came from books.

Heather

I learned from kids in the neighborhood and at school. In first or second grade, we would talk about what we thought names of different stuff was. I personally didn't know where babies came from. Our understanding of sex was that is was something done for pleasure.

Katherine

In sixth grade, boys and girls had their own sexual education class. Sixth grade was a time when we learned about body parts from diagrams. In eighth grade, I learned about sexual things from a classmate. His parents were divorced. When he went to his Dad's house, he watched Dr. Ruth on TV. He'd come back to school and tell a group of us what he learned about orgasms and blow jobs.

Each of the Coles had different experiences regarding sexual awareness. With the exception of Emily, everyone recalled friends at school being the first to educate them on sexuality. Emily began learning from romance novels, and she is the only one among her sisters who mentions asking a parent about sexuality. Mrs. Cole was raised in an environment and time when people did not talk about sexuality or ask questions. The childhood differences between Mrs. Cole and her oldest daughter, Emily, reflect the change in our society from the 1950s to the 1970s. American culture became more comfortable talking about and expressing sexuality. This is evident by Katherine's childhood experience during the 1980s. She is 10 years younger than Emily and heard her peers discussing oral sex and orgasms by the eighth grade.

Meet the Walkers

Mrs. Walker, Paul and Patricia have similar views but different experiences. The Walker women were very pleasant and talkative throughout their interviews. Out of all the Peterson siblings, Mrs. Walker disclosed the most information about her life. I believe she shares more personal information than most women in her age group would. Mrs. Walker took her time answering the questions. If she did not have other time commitments, I believe we could have spent the entire night talking at the table in her living room.

Patricia's interview took place at her home. We sat at the table in her dining room. She appeared to enjoy answering the questions. I believe her concerns as a mother raising a young boy allowed her to connect with the discussion differently from the other women in the Peterson family.

Her older brother, Paul, was the least talkative and the most reserved of the Walkers and of the extended Peterson family. We sat in the living room of his mother's home while she was at work. In line with his uncle, Mr. Cole, and his cousin, Katherine Cole, Paul had the television on too. Television can be a way for people to put up barriers. Mr. Cole and his daughter, Katherine, eventually connected with me and gave me their undivided attention. This did not happen with Paul. I felt some emotional distance from him that was not present before we began the interview. The television appeared to serve as the perfect escape route when I asked more personal questions. Our journey with the Walkers also begins with the question, *"Where did you receive your first messages about sexuality?"*

WALKER FAMILY

Mrs. Walker
I would say it was in the fourth grade. During school, two girls and two guys were talking about how a man and woman would get close. Gonorrhea and syphilis were also being discussed. My peers

were very sexually active. A lot of things that I heard
from them I had never heard before.

Paul
   I would have to say I learned about sex from
television. Around 14 or 15, there was lot of
gossiping between kids.

Patricia
   Starting around eighth grade, I received messages
about sexuality from my Mom, friends at school and
movies.

The Walker family's recollections are more general than the Coles.
It is amazing that Mrs. Walker personally knew fourth graders who
were sexually active during the 1950s. It makes one ponder what
circumstances and experiences led those children to become sexually
active at such an early age. If fourth grade children were having sex
during that time, I wondered, "Imagine what children without
education and guidance are doing today?"

Meet the Ryans

The Ryan Family was the very opposite of the Walker Family in
that the men talked more than Mrs. Ryan. Mr. Ryan and Otis were
more direct in comparison to the other men within the extended
Peterson family. Mr. Ryan and Otis' interviews took place over the
phone. Otis was very comfortable answering the questions while Mr.

Ryan sometimes hesitated before giving an answer. I encouraged Mr. Ryan to give his honest opinion, even if he didn't think other people would agree with him.

Mrs. Ryan's interview took place in the basement of her home. She spoke slowly and was relaxed throughout the interview. She hesitated only when questions were asked about the possibility of sexual abuse within her family. Mrs. Ryan is the only sibling in the Peterson family who did not have any daughters. This makes her experience as a mother unique in comparison to her sisters and brother.

The Ryans began their thoughtful exploration in our discussion by answering the first question, *"Where did you receive your first messages about sexuality?"*

RYAN FAMILY

Mrs. Ryan

I started hearing about it [sex] from friends at elementary school. The girls who were more advanced than I would tell me some of the things they had tried. Still, I didn't have a really good understanding of what they were talking about. Mom would only say so much. But I still wouldn't always understand. You advanced when you wanted to learn a little bit more about what they [friends] were saying. Somewhere along the line, I began to think, *"What does this [sex] mean exactly? How are you supposed to feel? How do you know about this [sex]?"* In the back of my mind, I heard when my mother used to say, *"Keep your dress down. Don't let the boys do this or that."* I heard this at a very early age. In the back of my mind this message was always there. I guess I would say I'm slow and still naïve about some things. Even now, I haven't experienced some of the things my friends would talk about.

Mr. Ryan
I learned about sex from other guys while playing at the ballpark. I was seven or eight years old.

Otis
When I was around six, I was fondling and playing around with a peer. I remember bumping into a certain area and getting a certain sensation because it was the private area.

All members of the Ryan family mention that they learned about sexuality from peers at an early age. Mrs. Ryan heard other girls talking about their sexual experiences. Mr. Ryan says he learned from male peers, although he does not say if this was through verbal communication, observation or a physical experience. Otis reveals that he actually experienced a sensation in the genital area when he had physical contact with another peer. Co-editor and contributing author, Dr. Donna Gaffney writes in *Adolescent Sexual Development and Sexuality*, that it is normal to begin experimenting with non-intercourse sexual behavior between the ages of nine and fourteen.[3] (Also see Chapter 4, regarding children and sexual curiosity.)

Meet David Peterson

Mr. Peterson was interviewed at a relative's house while no one was home. He was fairly jovial and appeared to not take the interview too seriously. His disposition changed when I asked personal questions related to his family. Mr. Peterson spoke at times with a lot of emotion. At other times, it appeared as if past memories were triggered even though he did not share what was on his mind. Of the four Peterson siblings, he's the only one who has children under 18. If I had been able to interview Mr. Peterson's estranged wife, I believe I would have gained a clearer picture of his immediate family. His brief answer to the first question, "*Where did you receive your first messages about sexuality?*" is where we began.

<u>Mr. Peterson</u>
At nine, I started hearing sexual things from friends.

What "sexual things" were children saying when Mr. Peterson was nine years old? Mr. Peterson is almost 20 years younger than his siblings. It would have been helpful to compare the sexual information his sisters received in the early 1950's to what he heard in the early 1970's if he had remembered what his peers said.

Chapter 2

Family Influence

In the previous chapter, we've noted that most members of the Peterson family mentioned learning about sexuality from friends at school or in their neighborhoods. Emily Cole is the only person who mentioned seeking out parental advice. Apparently, when parents and guardians do not communicate with their children, the latter can begin to explore and define their sexuality with inaccurate information and myths handed down by others. How much of a role should parents play? This is a question worth addressing.

The messages we receive from those closest to us greatly effect how we come to believe we should think, feel and behave in the world. Members of the Peterson family have varied memories about their childhoods. Some were given direct verbal statements about sexuality while others were ignored when they asked questions. The Coles, Walkers, Ryans and David Peterson all highlight the impact a family has in developing a child's perception of his/her sexuality. Note the answers to the questions below.

What messages did you receive from your family about sexuality?

How have the messages you received from your family affected the way you express your sexuality in the past and present?

COLE FAMLY

<u>Mrs. Cole</u>

When I was growing up, sexuality was not talked about at all in our house, so you really didn't understand it. I didn't see anyone kiss. But you knew by the way Mom and Dad spoke to each other they cared. It wasn't all about actually seeing them show affection. There are a lot of us [my siblings] here, so you have to have that [affection and love] before you go to the next step [having sex].

There were many myths out there, and I believed them. You didn't know the truth about anything. I found out the truth from experience. I would talk about kissing and things like that with my cousins, Stephanie and Janet. I thought French kissing was very awful. I thought, *"Eww, how can you do that? Put your tongue in somebody else's mouth!"* As far as at home, I didn't have any messages. We'd [my sisters] go out together and discuss whatever we could because, you have to see what is going on before you can come up with a question about something. One time, I remember saying, *"Eww, I don't know why everybody wants to kiss! There's nothing to kissing. You don't get anything out of kissing. At least I don't. Maybe there is something wrong with me"* [laughing]. I remember having that discussion.

Because sex wasn't talked about in the home, sometimes you were afraid. But at the same time,

when you experienced it, you are being a woman.
You're not letting your feelings run away with you or
being wild. You're just doing what you feel, or what
I feel God wants me to do... I'm not a big leader; I'm
a follower. Meaning, I am not a person who is going
to start any kind of sexual engagement if that makes
sense.

<u>Mr. Cole</u>
   As a boy, I was taught my sisters were delicate
because they were girls. You treated them differently
and looked at them as females. But it was different
from the way you would treat females in society
you'd possibly be romantic with. Since I was the
youngest and only boy in the household, I looked at
females in society differently because they were
potential girlfriends, wives or whatever.

<u>Emily</u>
   "I bet you betta not!" That was the message I
received from my family. We [my siblings] didn't
have any reference to sexuality. The act [sex] is
meant to do when you're married. It was always cut
and dry around sex. You wait until you're married.
There were no messages about pregnancy or sex
education. You just needed to leave that alone—
period. There was no doubt. I wasn't able to talk to
boys on the phone. By eighth grade, a couple boys
started to call. Dad's response was, *"We ain't tell you
that you could talk to boys yet."* As far as I'm
concerned, their message was, *"No. Don't even think
about it."*
   Youthfully, you knew it wasn't right—fuckin'
around, screwin', having real relationships. High
school age is when it would've been of interest to me.
I had little boyfriends and stuff but knew it wasn't

okay to be trying to do nothin'. I wasn't out screwin' around at that age, but I knew other people who were. I was still curious about it, but from what I was taught, it was not okay. Internally, I knew sex wasn't something idle you were just out there doing for the fun of it. That was the message my parents always delivered to me. My family had the feeling, *"You ain't supposed to be doing nothing until you are married."* It was easier for them to say. Thank goodness I somewhat listened.

I'm glad the earlier messages came from my family. Now it's less effective. I still know how my mom feels. If I brought home a male friend, they still won't say, *"Oh there's your room."* His room would be over here, and my room would be over there. That's exactly how Mom is going to conduct business. I still know in her mind she thinks, *"I don't care what you are doing on the West Coast. Here in Memphis, in my house, you're going to act like you don't know what sex is."* And to me that's a message too. Mom still says no unless you are settled down with that person. So I know what the message is. Most of the messages come from her. Dad probably agrees. But most of them come from her.

Heather
Sex was bad. *"You don't do nothing like that until you get married."* Or you heard, *"You can't watch that because it has sexual content in it."* Mom bought us books, but she never really talked about it. She said it was something that happens between two married people.

When I was younger, I just wanted to experiment. In the back of my head, I didn't pay attention to what my parents taught me. Now, my friends are like, *"You are getting old. You need to have a child."* I'm like, *"Uh uh! There is no way I'm having a child without being married."* During teenage and college years, my parents' message didn't play a part. But now, what they taught me and how they raised me is how I feel about sex. You get more mature and responsible.

Katherine
Mom bought a book when I was 11 or 12. It may have been called, *How We Are One*. It was about male and female sexual organs. In 11th grade, we had another sexual education class. I didn't know the answers for the test, so I went to Mom. She acted like she didn't know anything. So then, me and Heather went to Dad. The messages I received from Mom and Dad didn't affect my expression. Society affected me more.

Though Mrs. Cole did not receive any sexual messages in the home, we will later see how this varies from sibling to sibling. Growing up, Mrs. Cole believed the sexual myths she picked up because no one educated her on what was fact versus fiction. In spite of the lack of correct information Mrs. Cole had access to, she thinks not having this knowledge was better than where we are as a society today.

A sexual myth is an inaccurate, false statement believed to be true about the act of sex or sexuality. One common myth prevalent during the 1950s and 1960s was that, *a virgin cannot get pregnant her first time having unprotected sexual intercourse*. This myth is completely false but its power still has an effect on our youth today. During the summer of 2004, I conducted a sexuality workshop with teenage girls at a foster care residential treatment center in New York. A few girls mentioned boys using the *first time virgin* myth to get them to feel comfortable having sex with them. Some girls also inquired about the validity of this myth during our discussion of pregnancy and birth control.

Mrs. Cole's beliefs and upbringing influenced how she raised and educated her daughters. Since she believed in many sexual myths as a young person, I was surprised that Mrs. Cole did not become more knowledgeable so that she could pass on the correct information to her daughters. When Katherine asked for help on her sexual education test, she was unable to assist her. Emily says that even though she is an adult in her 40s, Mrs. Cole would not allow her and a significant other to share the same bed in their house. Her mother's belief that marriage is the only environment where sex between two people is appropriate has not wavered.

Despite what an individual's spiritual or religious beliefs are, it would greatly benefit families to expand their understanding of sexuality beyond the act of sex. Awareness of ourselves as sexual beings begins well before two people decide to marry. Another contributing author and editor in *Adolescent Sexual Development and Sexuality*, Dr. Carol Roye, defines puberty as: a period of physiological change during or before adolescence, by which a child is transformed into a young adult.[4] Puberty usually begins sooner for

African American children than white children. It can begin as early as age nine for girls, and nine and a half for boys. Dr. Roye also states, more researchers are accepting age seven as a normal time of breast development in girls.

Families can raise and educate children without putting a negative stigma on sexuality and sex. If a child is taught that sex is "bad", as Heather was, what do they subconsciously think of themselves once they learn sex is the way in which they were created to come into the world?

WALKER FAMILY

<u>Mrs. Walker</u>

I can't hardly remember. Sex was something we couldn't talk about at home. Usually, if you mentioned anything about sex in the house, it was dropped like you didn't say anything. So a lot of things that I learned, I learned from peers out there in the street. I can't say television because we didn't have a television. Can't say books because I didn't get my hands on any books at that particular time engaging in any type of sexuality. So I'd probably have to honestly say when I was almost pregnant with Paul is when I started learning.

You know, sexuality is something we very seldom talk about. I don't know if it's because of how we were brought up that it's something we don't talk about as adults. Not receiving any messages had a great effect on me. It's like doing a job without any tools. I felt, if I knew more about sexuality growing up, I could have understood a lot more instead of jumping into the fire blind. I didn't know anything during my first experience. When it came to the time when people would say, *"You are now a young lady after you start your period,"* I never knew what they meant. To be honest with you, that weighed on me very heavily for a long time. I just found out as an adult what that really means, *"Once you start your period you can become pregnant."* I never could connect the two together. Never even knew what it meant to *"become a young lady."* Nobody would explain things to you, but you'd hear people say things. So if nobody would tell you stuff, it was very hard unless you heard if from somebody out in the street.

Certain things were just very embarrassing. If you had a little bit of information, you had something to work with. I had a real strong resentment towards my mother because I felt like she should have taught us certain things about sexuality as far as growing up and being a young lady. Just giving you a rag and saying, *"Use this,"* you don't understand anything behind that. You don't know how long you're going to stay on. You don't know that when you start your period you can become pregnant. I felt like I could listen to other people talk, but I couldn't contribute anything because I didn't know anything. I don't know about the rest of my sisters and brother, but it really caused a lot of hardship for me. I felt like if I knew more, I would not have gotten pregnant. Maybe I would have. Even if I did, I would have had some type of tools to work with.

I never knew when you were a virgin, if you had sex for the first time, you could become pregnant. That was my first time. I heard people say you could not get pregnant the first time. These were people older than me. They weren't distant relatives. Maybe they were some relatives we didn't claim because they were so far down the line. Anyway, they were older than me and I overheard certain things. So when the time came for me, I never thought I could get pregnant because I knew I had never done anything before. So, sure enough I went out, and when I did it, became pregnant. I never knew I was pregnant because I didn't know exactly what occurred afterwards. Even after I was pregnant, I didn't know how you had a baby. I thought when you had a baby it would come out of the rectum. I never knew a baby came out of your vagina until it was almost time for me. I guess I was six or seven months pregnant when I found out, and I just couldn't believe it. It completely freaked me out.

I was sitting in the kitchen and kept asking my mother, *"Mom, how is this gonna take place? Do you have to squat?"* She said, *"It's coming out the same way it went in."* I still couldn't put the two together. *"It came out the same way it went in. It came out the same way it went in."* I kept saying it over and over to myself and it didn't make any sense. Finally, it clicked. When it clicked, I had a real hard time dealing with that. I was so scared. I was so frightened because, in my whole life, I never knew where babies came from. So here I am pregnant and thinking a baby comes from somewhere else. I was 16 almost 17 and never understood how I got pregnant, to be honest with you. It brought a whole lot of hardship. A lot of things would have been different.

Today, I don't hold anything against my mom. Since I've been an adult, I now talk to my mom and make her answer certain questions she would never talk about when we were coming up. It was hard for me when I sat down and talked to her on several different occasions. It really broke my heart to learn she never told us anything because she didn't know. Her parents didn't tell her anything. So it began to make sense why she didn't tell us anything or why she couldn't. That hurt me to hear her tell her story. Everything began to connect. The puzzle finally began to fit. I felt sorry for her too. I really did. I said to myself, *"Wow. Here she is with four kids and she didn't know anything either."*

Paul

I think the big sex talk came from my mom. I can't say exactly when—probably the general age of 16. By me being older, I see stuff a lot different as far as females. It's just me, my mom and my sister. I see stuff my sister goes through and stuff I go through. I would say I'm getting somewhat more mature, as far as relating to females.

Patricia

I was told by my mom to wait to have sex until I was completely sure—be sure I was "in love" with the boy; it's something that you can never get back and be careful about getting pregnant. I'd have to say, watching your aunts and how they developed over the years kinda helped you display your sexuality along the lines of how they matured. I know if I was going to a family function, I wouldn't want to be caught in a crop or bra top and panty shorts. I don't have any aunties who I've ever seen dress like that. So I guess you kinda look at them as role models in some way. You try to follow along with that—look like a lady and carry yourself in a certain way.

Mrs. Walker's lack of education had such a profound impact on her that she became pregnant as a teenager. By not talking within our

30

families and with our children directly, we send out the message that sexuality is something shameful and secretive. Mrs. Walker's experience determined how she would educate her daughter. Patricia can recall precisely the information she received from her mother while Paul, on the other hand, is very vague in his description of sexual messages.

If Mrs. Walker had someone in her life to talk with or educate her about the risk of pregnancy and unprotected sex, Paul may have been born when Mrs. Walker was mature enough to handle pregnancy and the birth of a child. Her experience as a teenager illustrates the power a sexual myth can have in young person's life without the proper guidance and access to information.

RYAN FAMILY

Mrs. Ryan

I guess I could say me and my sisters would talk about sexuality. We would talk on what we were wondering about and what we were picking up from other friends. At the same time, we still didn't quite understand it. Further on down the road, as you grew older, you heard certain things. Sometimes you were still not at ease because you still hadn't experienced sex yourself. I would say I was still kinda naïve. Even if you were hearing sexual things you thought, *"I don't know about this,"* because it may work for other people, and it may not work for me. This was in elementary school but you still wondered. And then some messages came from my mom.

I would say my mom's messages really stuck to me. It was rooted in you even though you didn't fully understand. It follows you. And when you grow older, you understood things were said because it would keep you out of trouble.

Mr. Ryan

I was only raised by my mother. She was always against approaching women sexually. When I was 11, she started telling me to leave girls alone when she saw us playing house. Older female cousins would also tell me about sex. Back when I was young, I wasn't nice to women. Now I give respect to women no matter what they look like.

Otis

I got the message that if one has experienced the accidental bump in the wrong area creating arousal—curiosity is okay. The person I did this with was a cousin. As you continue to play, whether it's the opposite or same sex, if you experience that arousal, it will stay on your mind. You don't know whether to go to Mom or Dad because someone bumped you in a certain way and it felt good. You didn't know it was wrong. I had my first conversation with a peer before an adult. I could talk to him. Messages from adults came through listening and viewing how my mom and dad were. I didn't see a lot of cuddling and kissing.

I don't know if it was the peer situation or the situation with my cousin where I found out it was wrong. There was a situation with a cousin or my brother where we were in the back seat petting each other. I was between six and eight years old. One of my parents saw us and swatted at us with their hand while saying, *"What are ya'll doing?!"* Family experiences back then didn't affect me to the point where it affects me now. There was no education from my immediate house. It was at school and peers.

Mrs. Ryan still did not have a clear idea of what sexuality was after discussing it with her sisters. Mrs. Cole and Mrs. Walker were not in the position to help her because their peers were the only people talking about sexuality. Perhaps this is why Mrs. Ryan did not pass down any information to her oldest son. If Otis' parents had educated him, maybe he would have felt comfortable talking to them about his first sexual experiences. There are many innocent behaviors and experiences that occur between children who are related to each other. But there are also many instances where the behavior is callous, particularly with teenagers sexually molesting younger children. Otis' feelings and behaviors could have been acknowledged and discussed without making him feel embarrassed.

Mr. Ryan stated his mother raised him. For parents to simply tell a child to stay away from the opposite sex when they see the child doing something they do not like, as his mother did, is not enough. If children are not clear why they should stay away from someone, why would they stop? Parents and guardians usually express unclear messages and warnings out of concern for their children's safety. A better approach would be to sit down and have a discussion with a child, using language appropriate to the child's age, truthfully answering any questions the child asks. This method could have been used with Otis versus swatting him. Honest communication should begin during the time the child begins to learn language so that there'll be no embarrassing situations later.

DAVID PETERSON

<u>Mr. Peterson</u>
I never received any education from my family. Never! It didn't affect me at all, as far as not receiving any information from them because I was never given any. It hurt me a lot but I learned to get over it.

Based on Mr. Peterson's contradictory statement, not receiving basic sexuality education from his family did have an effect on him. He felt hurt and most likely confused. I speculate he did his best to educate himself after not receiving any answers from his family. Perhaps he tried to get clarity from family members on a situation, and to his disappointment, was not given the information he needed. One of the nation's leading experts on sexuality, Dr. Gail Elizabeth Wyatt, offers advice in her book *Stolen Women* by stating, "*Parents need to take a much more active role not only in offering guidance to their children on a continuous basis but in discussing any and all sexual topics that arise. If they do not, they may miss opportunities to reeducate their children and protect them from exploitation or abuse.*"[5]

Chapter 3

Sexualized Society

Do we create our environment or are we a product of it? In Chapter 2, we learned that the Peterson siblings did not receive very much guidance or information from their parents. I am sure this is reflected in the different time periods the Peterson siblings and their parents grew up. Mama and Papa Peterson were raised during the 1910s and 1920s and had very little knowledge to share with their children about sexuality. Unfortunately, this lack of knowledge affected their children and grandchildren. This is how different people and institutions outside of the home can become our children's teachers and largest influencers.

The social attitudes and expectations prevailing in the 1940s prevented adequate public discussion about anything sexual in nature. The beginning of a sexual revolution could be seen by the 1950s. By the 1960s, attitudes of free love and expression were strong, as young people of that generation began to reject the traditional values of their parents. Then, media started becoming a powerful socio-cultural institution, influencing our sexual attitudes in the 1970s. By the

1980s, many people thought things were getting completely out of hand with the spread of sexually transmitted diseases on the rise and our country's beginning awareness of HIV infection and AIDS.

Today, the landscape has changed in regards to the various public images of sexuality we see. Music, television, advertising and movies are much more sexually explicit than 20 to 40 years ago. These same industries show adolescents discovering their sexuality at earlier ages and adults engaging in same sex, heterosexual and bisexual behavior and relationships. Many people blame outside influences as the reason we have "lost our values and morals." Where did our values and morals originate? I wanted to know if the Petersons thought our society had an effect on sexuality in general and if the impact helped or hindered us. Notice here that each family has their own set of opinions and beliefs.

How do you think society influences sexuality?

How have the messages that you have received from society affected the way you express your sexuality, past and present?

COLE FAMILY

Mrs. Cole
TV influences society very much. I think it's outrageous the way things are now. There is nothing left to your imagination. It's all right there for you. I think when youngsters see sexuality in that way, they

want to demonstrate or experience these things to see, *"What's so great about it? Why does everybody do it right out there in the open?"* I think it was better when you left it to the imagination. If you thought somebody was about to kiss on TV, they took the picture away where you had to imagine what could have happened afterwards. You didn't have to see it right there before your eyes.

Music is another influence. I think the way people dress is another influence. I don't think this generation has gone as far as someone screaming or saying vulgar things or doing sexual gestures towards other people. This generation does express sexuality in a certain way. Perverts usually do the vulgar things. Advertisements are an influence. Sex is all over the place. It's not hidden anymore. Back then, there wasn't anything. You just went with your feelings. Perhaps whoever your partner was led you to the next step. But for me there wasn't anything to see.

Now, I don't think society influences me anyway whatsoever because I think about the religious side of it—what's right and what's bad, keeping it clean and not getting kinky with it. Clean is the way God wants us to make love, I think. Not some of this kinky stuff they do. I don't know what all of it is, but I do know there is some kinky stuff going on. I'm clean with it, holding, caressing, kissing and intercourse—the proper way. Nobody is going to be lifting me up in an elevator like they do in the movies [laughing]. That's what I mean. I'm not going to be on top of a piano like in [the movie] *An Officer and a Gentleman*. Those are kinky. It's not exactly kinky but those are far out ways. I'm not into far out ways.

Mr. Cole

We treat women with respect since they are the weaker sex. Just by God putting them on earth, we treat them differently. You support and protect them. But the biggest societal influence is clothes. Women's shopping is a societal thing. They are given different choices. Women are different and they like to shop. A man's fashion and style is set. Women change, and the way they dress is a sexual thing. Women like to show off, I guess.

Emily

Society influences sexuality tremendously by giving the cues as to whether or not it's good or bad. It's outrageous. It's too much now. Back in the olden days when I was a little kid, late 60s early 70s, you didn't see anything on TV about sex. If innuendoes or certain references were made in certain programming, it was very limited. You got the impression they were saying something, but nothing was spelled out. Now it's not only spelled out, it's drawn, written, *everything*. It's everywhere. It's overabundant now to a point where I'm thinking, *"You can keep that stuff!"* Or society's almost saying too much when it's not even necessary to divulge that much information.

I always felt you are as strong as your friends are. I had good friends. They were really good girls and respected themselves. Even if they didn't know what they wanted, they knew they weren't there to be one of the girls the guys were gonna go through. We talked about sex a lot. Even if I was ever thinking about it, one of my girlfriends would say, *"Are you sure? Do you REALLY want to?"* They influenced me probably more than my parents did at that age, when it was really crucial. If they had all been out there doing their thing as young ladies, I might have been more open to it.

I would hate to be a kid now. I would hate to be younger and impressionable. We didn't have the music videos and stuff when I was coming up. So I wouldn't have had the same messages they get with the girls' booties hanging out. I don't appreciate the relations they show on TV—period. You know, the guys being mack daddy and the girls struttin' around and stuff. I think that's tacky. It gives the same impression to me, as far as sexuality. That's what women are to men as far as what's described in the video—objects.

In general you know how people talk. *"You settle down and find yourself a good guy,"* is what we say to women. Guys can be whatever. *"Find yourself a guy with money,"* is a message you can get in general from society or people you know personally. I wonder, *"What are the messages they give men?"* What do men look for in women? Is it face or body? I don't know. Some go by intelligence, intellect and stuff like that. I just think they grade women on such a lesser scale as to what men should be seeking in us. Men aren't on the same scale as we are.

To me, sexuality is not a sacred thing in our society anymore. For some people, it still is. For the ones that act like it's sacred, I applaud them because even I don't. My general nature in discussing it amongst friends and co-workers is very open. It's not anything secretive. I can recall a time when it was.

I'm not even through with this question! Let's start talking about the "mixing up." We can start talking about gays and all that too. That's outlandish now. There was a time when that was "behind the closets," as they would say. It ain't that way no more. *Queer Eye For The Straight Guy* [television show] is making it sound like its all good [snapping her fingers]. They are celebrities. They are popular, and I'm saying, *"Puhleeze!"* I have my own view about that kind of stuff. I think that's very personal. Do whatever you want but don't try to commercialize it. Don't try to act like that's the best thing for the world because I don't think that's the case. I think once they finalize same sex marriage... And I think it will happen against our best judgment. Once the same sex marriages come into play, society will change a whole other way regarding sexuality. When they have offspring from those relationships, I think society is going to change a lot. That's a decade or two down the road. Society won't look like it looks now. And to me, it looks out-of-hand now. It will really be Noah's Arc [biblical story] then. That's really my opinion. It's just really getting to a point where people are saying, *"That's okay."* I know everybody's opinion is different, but society is giving them more of a "thumbs up." Same sex relationships were very quiet and not supposed to have been the norm at one time. Society has changed it.

Now I don't give a damn what folks think. In terms of youthfulness, around high school age, I was probably more considerate of what I saw out in society. When I was younger, I was more open-minded. Things were cool. I didn't think people should be treated any differently because of their sexual preferences. It didn't have anything to do with society. That was my own thinking then. I just didn't think it was right. Growing up, I remember feeling more open-minded about stuff. Now I'm saying, *"People need to get a hold of themselves,"* because they are outrageous!

Living out on the West Coast, child, has opened my eyes to a lot of stuff. I think if I had not lived here, I would have never heard people talk about swingers and all that kind of stuff. I'm not saying people approach me that way. But there's nothing you can't get into that you'd want to here. This didn't exist 20 years ago, to my knowledge. Now it's no telling what you'll run across. Everything is out there—all kinds of weird stuff. I call it weird because I don't understand or know anything about it. I don't know... I guess I'm not that free or open. I guess I'm one of the stauncher people now. I'm not gonna say things are wrong. I just have my own view.

<u>Heather</u>
Media, magazines and TV have affected me. It's like the flesh is weak. There was this voice saying, *"Heather, you're gonna regret this."* TV and society makes it seem like casual sex is okay. They made me think it was okay. It wasn't like that when I was growing up. Eighty percent of society and different media contribute to this. Because of my morals and values, I don't see it like that. At first, I used to have sex. Now I'm gonna wait until I get married. God says you are not supposed to have casual sex. I guess how I was raised is coming back.

<u>Katherine</u>
I think advertising, magazines and TV commercials promote sex with sexual pictures. Back in the old days, I don't remember seeing sex in shows. Now they leave nothing to the imagination. Advertisement gives females messages that it's okay to be sexually active at an earlier age. They promote sex negatively.

It's a trip how guys are overprotective of girls or their younger sisters when they were after girls the same way young boys are today... I only had sex for the curiosity of it, knowing it wasn't going to be good. I don't see the point of casual sex. It's supposed to be with the person you love. That's why I'm waiting until I'm married. I think sex is overrated.

I feel I'm an old head. I think I'm a prude and naïve to sexual things. I think society influences it in a harmful way. I didn't know about sex at a young early age. When people say they lost their virginity at 14, I think, *"What the fuck?!"* I don't feel people should just hand it over. I think sex is a gift.

Sometimes I think everyone is doing it and feel I should do it because everyone else is. But I believe people should wait until they get married. I don't think I'm modest. Yet, I don't express my sexuality at all. Society shows skinny hoes and makes me not want to show my sexuality because I'm fat. The older I get, I might wanna show a little cleavage, but I'll never show a leg.

The women in the Cole family share similar views regarding the impact society has on sexuality. Mrs. Cole and her daughters feel that American culture has gone overboard with the quantity and quality of sexual messages that are put out by the media. Mr. Cole addresses the culture's influence only in relation to women. Pointing out that women like to show off and shop, he ignores who and what influences women to want to dress sexually and buy the latest trends. Women's fashions have evolved with the idea that a woman should dress in a manner that is sexually desirable to men. The only person who addresses the impact society has had on both sexes is Emily. She believes the different messages society gives men and women causes women to be "graded on a lesser scale."

All of the Cole women mention God as the teacher on how they are supposed to conduct themselves sexually. Mrs. Cole believes there is a proper way that God wants people to have sex. "Far out" or "kinky" ways would be contradictory to that. At one time, Emily was more open-minded, but now she judges aspects of sexuality she does not agree with, such as same sex marriages. Heather used to think casual sex was okay, and now she does not. Katherine shares the same sentiments as her sister, Heather, declaring that she will not have sex again until she is married. What changed their minds?

We have come to a point in our culture where unless a person is married, satisfying a sexual desire is labeled as "weak"; remaining abstinent is considered an example of strength. Not every single person in the Peterson family agrees with this. However, it would appear that more women in the Peterson family, like the larger society, share beliefs similar to the Cole women on this subject.

Women face a dilemma between what is expected of them versus how they feel inside. I have met women who have labeled themselves as "born again virgins" until they find a suitable man to partner with again. A renewed allegiance to their religious faith usually arises out of frustration from failed relationships. This action alone rarely solves women's problems, reflecting a deeper issue. Learning to negotiate the need of being in a sexually fulfilling relationship, married or not, can be difficult depending on the expectations of the dominant socio-cultural institution in a woman's life. It is evident that religion is the leading force in the lives of the Cole women.

Katherine does not see herself as a sexually attractive woman because of the images she sees in American culture. Does she really believe premarital sex is wrong because of her religious beliefs or is it her self-esteem? Many women compare their sexual attractiveness to unrealistic images of women in mainstream media. In September 2004, Dove's beauty and skin care products launched their *Campaign for Real Beauty* in an effort to challenge society's stereotypical definition of beauty and attractiveness. In June 2005, Dove featured six women from size four to twelve (not models) in their commercial advertising. More initiatives such as these are needed to counter unrealistic images of women in the media and help women develop and maintain positive body images and healthy self esteem.

WALKER FAMILY

Mrs. Walker

I think they influence sexuality by the way women dress. I know people have a right to wear what they want to wear but some things people wear are very degrading. That's my personal opinion. They may not see it like that. I think they advertise too much sex on TV. In any type of advertisement or commercial, you always see a female present. If they are trying to sell a car, a female is somewhere in the background. Society makes being female very degrading. Because of this, men don't look at you in a ladylike way or even a womanly way. A lot of that comes from television. It comes from off of the street, and it could be in the home too. But I honestly think TV has the biggest influence on degrading females. In women's magazines you often see a woman not dressed completely. She has to be showing off some part of her body.

I remember seeing a film on sex in elementary school. It was about your menstrual cycle. The boys could not come in. It was strictly for girls at that time. Even though I saw the film, I didn't know exactly what it was pertaining to. I was still dumbfounded and didn't know anything. That takes me back to when I first started my period. I didn't know what it was. I remember my teacher wrote down "Kotex" on a piece of paper, told me to go to the store and ask somebody to show me where it was. I did as she told me. I'll never forget it. It was A & P Grocery Store. I went and looked myself because I was too embarrassed to ask a cashier. You'll laugh but it's the truth. I looked in the all fruits and vegetables—the produce department. I couldn't find it. I was picking up apples and oranges, looking for it. I left the store without anything.

When I went back to school the next day, the teacher asked me had I found it. I told her the store didn't have it. She asked me, *"Where did you look?"* I told her, *"I looked in the vegetable and fruit section."* She said, *"No, take the paper and give it to a cashier."* I did do that and came home with a bag of Kotex. But I was so embarrassed to even buy them in a store. I was looking around, hoping nobody was in front or back of me. I was nervous. I didn't want anybody to see me. I felt like it was something dirty. The reason I felt like it was something dirty was because it was something we could never talk about at home. I just assumed it was something filthy you couldn't talk about, because when it was talked about sex was something nasty, filthy, and you didn't do it.

I feel like I can really talk about sexuality now and not feel bad about it. I have learned a lot of things on my own. The things I feel now are how I feel and not what someone told me. Even if I see sex on TV, I have my own thoughts now. To me, everything you do or everywhere you go, you learn something, whether it's sexuality or something else. Nine times out of ten, it's going to be sexuality or have something to do with it. I would say books, watching dirty movies, talking about sex openly, having my ears open and listening to other people talk about it were ways I learned. A lot of times, other people talked about sex and made it seem dirty. I looked at sexuality and viewed it differently. I felt like it wasn't anything dirty. After being an adult, you look at a lot of things differently, and it changes you as a whole person. A lot of that has to do with how *I* feel about things spiritually. I know sexuality is not dirty because if it was God wouldn't have given us certain feelings. He gave sexual feelings to us, but it's supposed to be intact. Basically, that's where I received my own thinking and thoughts.

Paul

Sex sells. Everything is based on some shape or form of sex. Whether it's buying or selling something, commercials on TV or whatever, it always has something to do with sex. Society plays a big part in it. If that was not the case, there would be a lot of out-of-work bikini models. And there wouldn't be a lot of magazines. I'm even guilty of that, but I buy magazines for the cars because I'm a car nut. Whether it's a car or motorcycle magazine, they always have some sexual reference in it.

I don't think I really express my sexuality. Having sex is different. How I interact and deal with women doesn't have anything to do with society. Those are my own personal experiences. Every female is different. So you can't base how you treat somebody else off of what society thinks. They don't have an impact on me.

Patricia

I think society influences sexuality a lot through fashion and the style of clothes. These young girls are dressing like "video girls" in junior high, which is making them start having sex at a younger age. I would say movies made me curious. When you are young and see a man and woman humpin', sweatin' and looking like they are having such a great time you're like, *"Wow! I like a boy too. I wanna do that."* So I think movies add a lot. That's why they say the TV can really mess your kids' heads up.

Society has had a lot of influence on me—a lot! Let's start with religion. Religion kinda keeps you discreet. That's the good side of it. For example, when you are going to a formal dinner, you wear formal clothes; that's the religious side coming out. You know when and where to be a lady. On the other hand, you have TV, which shows you the sexy side of a woman. Every once in a while you want to be sexy. Your friends you go to the club with are influencing you, saying, *"Girl, you should take that off the shoulder a little bit."* Then there are your parents. Whenever I would go out, my mom would have to see what I had on. While checking me up and down, I'd hear, *"Oh that's too short! I don't like that,"* or *"That's fine."* So religion keeps you discreet

about certain things, says how to act and behave.
Then sometimes you get a little wild. I would have to
say the wild side comes more from friends and the
media. Still, a little bit within yourself comes out.

The Walkers all stated that society influences women's sexuality
through their appearance. For instance, Mrs. Walker says women are
constantly used in commercials and advertising. Her son, Paul, uses
the example of women being used to sell cars in magazines. Patricia
refers to young girls wearing clothes to express themselves. Clothes
alone do not make girls want to have sex at a younger age. The
fashion industry is responsible for making clothes and the provocative
messages they promote to young girls in order to entice them to buy
the latest fashion trends. Mainstream, commercial music videos also
help advertise and support these unhealthy images.

Paul does not think he expresses his sexuality, even though he has
sex. Having sex is a part of expressing one's sexuality. Patricia
believes the role religion serves in keeping a person discreet is a good
thing. Discretion can be healthy in some situations and disastrous in
others. Religions advocating sexual repression as the only path to
purity are no better than mainstream media giving youth a green light
to engage in sexual behavior with no responsibility or control. They
are both distortions of our sexuality. There is a healthy "middle
ground" our children could benefit from learning. It would be to our
advantage to teach our children messages of healthy expression, pride

and respect of self and others instead of teaching them from a place of fear.

RYAN FAMILY

<u>Mrs. Ryan</u>

Well, I think TV would be number one. They talk about sex and show certain things. The next would be certain magazines. I think too much is going on now—too much. Things could be taken out of TV and some of the magazines.

When we were younger, we didn't have the full understanding of sex compared to the way it is today. Sometimes, when you stop and think, it seems like they make things more dirty, and it's really not about that. The outside world and society plays with a lot of things. If two people are in love, there is nothing bad about sex. But then again, it's not a game. Sex is not something you go out and do or talk about all the time. Don't assume you can go up to somebody else and touch or talk about what you're going to do or how you're going to do it to them. That goes on today. Sex is a clean thing in more ways than one. Even growing up, you had questions about sex, *"Why do you have to do this? Why is it done this way? Why is it that way?"* Still sometimes you question these things and you wonder, *"God, dog, that don't seem right. That's nasty!"*

<u>Mr. Ryan</u>

Society influences sexuality by the way women dress and talk. Women reveal their navels, and now they aren't wearing bras! In general, they reveal too much in order to get someone to notice them. It starts at an early stage now—like 12 or 13 They smoke too. To a certain extent, society affected me learning how to approach a woman. I noticed people approach girls in a disrespectful way, depending on how the girl acted.

Otis

Society influences sexuality a whole lot. It depends on how far they go. TV gives its side. It shows exposed skin on the body. Things began to change when the world progressed with women wanting rights, freedom, and them being able to do what men do. Women changed what they wanted to wear before things really changed in society. This sparked off into sexuality. Women wanted to shed more clothes and other people wanted to make money, regardless of the drawbacks that came with how it was represented.

Man has a little ego thing going back to the days of Eve and Christ [biblical reference]. I think men believe women are here for a certain reason regarding sexuality. I'm not sure what that is. I don't know if a woman's bone structure or physically being weaker made her want to stay home with the kids. Men think they have certain rights. Some men expect their wives to be laying up waiting for them when they get home. This comes from certain laws and the Bible. Men in society watch how other men act towards their women. So they think its okay to treat women in certain ways.

Society didn't affect me in a positive or negative way. I don't see positivity in sexuality anyway. It seems to be too much for the mind until it's mature enough to comprehend. This maturity happens around 11 or 13 years old. Society has a *big* impact on me now because you see what's wrong and you see what's right. A man was put here for a woman and a woman was put here for a man. When you know you came here from conception, you start forming an image of what that is. You think about a woman at a certain age and you want to learn how to treat them, cater to them and love them. You learn emotional needs need to be met 50/50.

Mrs. Ryan again admits she did not have a full understanding of sexuality when she was growing up. Today, she feels there is too much displayed on television and in magazines. Mr. Ryan displays a clear bias towards women. When asked about society's influence on sexuality, he focused only on the outer appearance of women. There is no mention of how men are influenced or what they are responsible for.

In general, the Petersons primarily discussed today's younger generation and women when asked about society and sexuality. When Otis was asked to comment on the influence society has on sexuality, his focus included men and made the point of tracing sexism and the ownership of women back to the Bible. Religion can shape how people express and suppress their sexuality. Otis believes that men's expectation of their wives to be sexually available comes from the Bible. His opinion has value. Genesis, chapter three, versus 16 in the King James version of the Bible reads as follows: "Unto the woman he said, I will greatly multiply thy sorrow and thy conception; in sorrow thou shalt bring forth children; and thy desire shall be to thy husband, and he shall rule over thee."[6]

Otis also gave a valid example in reference to women's fashion. Despite the importance of the Women's Rights Movement, Otis thinks the drawback in fashion was making money off women wanting to "shed more clothes." The Women's Rights Movement and feminism dealt with a lot more than clothes. The second-wave of feminism, beginning in the 1960s, largely focused on issues of equality, discrimination and oppression. Still Otis' opinion has some merit. The money made from objectifying women in fashion and other industries has become the focal point regardless of how these images are projected and the impact they have on society.

Mr. Ryan supports Otis' opinion by stating that the larger portion of our society still labels a woman according to what she is wearing. He saw many women being disrespected due to how they carried themselves. Given his own admission of not being nice to women in Chapter 2, it is safe to assume Mr. Ryan also treated women with disrespect due to their appearance. However, he is not the only man guilty of this.

Judging a woman based on her clothing and appearance has also been used as a defense strategy by attorneys for men accused of sexual violence against women. These beliefs have spiraled out of control to where some child predators blame children for seducing them with what they are wearing. Bishop T. D. Jakes' powerful movie, *Woman Thou Art Loosed*, examines the effects of sexual abuse in the life of an African American woman. In one disturbing scene, the lead character remembers being 12 and accused by her mother's live in boyfriend of teasing him by wearing tight jeans. Later, when he rapes her, she is wearing a pretty flowing white dress.

Based on his own personal experience, Otis came to the conclusion that sexuality is too much for a child to handle. He disclosed having sexual interactions with one of his relatives and a peer in Chapter 2, but he did not say how old he was when this occurred. Learning about one's sexuality begins from birth. As newborns grow, they discover their own body parts and the sensations that naturally occur. As a toddler develops into a child, (s)he may innocently discover that certain body sensations are pleasurable. According to doctors at the Mayo Foundation for Medical Education and Research, by age three or four, children may examine each other to satisfy their curiosity and learn why they have different genitals.[7] They need to know this is a natural part of their sexual development and growth.

DAVID PETERSON

Mr. Peterson
I believe the TV should be cut down to a certain point because it influences kids too much. TV influences kids on sex and a lot of other things. While growing up, I grew up on my own. I grew on my own because I only had to deal with myself. I was very disappointed by my family.

Once again, Mr. Peterson mentions being frustrated with his family but does not elaborate on how or why they disappointed him. He seems to be saying that society did not impact his sexuality because he grew up on his own. Mr. Peterson remained unclear about where, how and when he learned about sexuality, given that he believes his family and social environment played no part in his growth and development.

When discussing sexuality, gender bias is often revealed. Women's sexual behavior is scrutinized more than men's. In order to determine where double standards began in the Peterson family, the next logical step was to find out how the parents taught their own children about sexuality and if there were different messages articulated to boys and girls based on gender.

Chapter 4

How Do We Raise
Sexually Aware Children?

The adult children of the Cole, Walker and Ryan families are in their 20s, 30s and 40s. I wanted to know how Mr. and Mrs. Cole, Mrs. Walker and Mr. and Mrs. Ryan educated them. The answers from their adult children let us know how effective or ineffective their parents' teachings were. Mr. Peterson is the only sibling in the Peterson family who has children under 18 years old. Since they were not interviewed, we are unable to make the same comparisons in his immediate family as we did with Mr. Peterson's siblings.

Mrs. Walker and her brother, Mr. Peterson, have children of both sexes. I was interested in evaluating if gender bias played a part in how they raised their sons as opposed to their daughters. The Cole parents and Mrs. Ryan played the "what if" game and contemplated what they would have done had they raised children of the opposite sex. Most importantly, I wanted to see how the adult children of the Peterson siblings are currently teaching their children. Therefore, Paul

Walker, Patricia Walker and Otis Peterson all gave input on how they were currently raising and educating their own children about sexuality.

If you have children, how did you teach them about sexuality? If you do not, how would you teach your children?

Would there be a difference between what you would teach your son versus your daughter if you had children of both sexes?

COLE FAMILY

<u>Mrs. Cole</u>

Hopefully, I started educating my kids at a pretty young age. By them going to Catholic school, I knew there were certain books I could get for them. I always made sure books were around, and we could talk at anytime. I definitely made sure they knew about their menstrual period when they were about to start. When I was young and found out, nobody told me about it, I thought something was wrong with me. It just so happened I was at home that particular day. I didn't feel well so I didn't go to school. So when it happened, I went to Mom to tell her something was wrong and asked, *"What do I do?"* I never wanted my kids to experience that. I was always available for them to ask questions. I don't know if I was the instigator. Sometimes I was, especially when they got older and started dating. I always asked them about what was going on. Before they dated, I didn't ask any questions unless they asked me.

There possibly would've been a difference if I had a son. I would have made sure he understood there are always consequences to having sex prematurely. On the other hand, I would have pushed him off on his Dad instead of me handling things. I don't think I would have gotten very deep with him. Maybe there are some things I don't understand as much as his father would about a boy's feelings and things like that. I would put that off for his Dad to discuss. I would tell a son about basic things, especially about getting a girl pregnant, how one thing leads to another and you have to be a responsible person.

Mr. Cole

Well, since the kids are all girls, I didn't have to teach them anything. Whatever questions they had about sexuality, like boy-girl attraction, I answered them as honestly as I could. Very few questions were taboo. But between a father and a daughter, there are one or two topics you could say is something the mother should answer. What girls go through when they reach a certain age, certainly things about having babies and how it happens, should be left to the mother. Other than that, if questions were about boys I was all open, and I was going to answer them. I think I could relate to relationships with boys—what to do and what not to do.

If I had a son, I would have given him the whole aspect of boyhood, manhood, girls and women, and anything I thought he may need to know to function in society. If he had any questions, I would have answered those. There wouldn't have been any taboo topics with a son. I would have told him how to treat girls and protect yourself. Particularly with girls and marriage, make sure you love them. I'd tell him there are certain steps: dating, fall in love and get married. During all of those, you treat women with respect.

Emily

Well, right now, it's not my intention to have any kids. If I did, I would teach them sex is still something of value more so because of safety factors. I wouldn't want them delving and venturing out there. You know things have changed. AIDS makes things different now. Just for their own safety, they would know all about that kind of stuff because I know how one message could be given. A kid is going to tell you one thing, but I want them to be knowledgeable about what they should be doing. If they are going to be out there tampering around, I'll tell them I understand they are going to be feeling the way they do. Just don't mess with it idly. Sex is not as important to other people. I don't think anybody indulges in sex idly if they have a good sense of themselves. That's how I'd talk to my kids. And I'd always make them feel like they are worth a lot—not just based around their sexuality though—in general. I would really try to impress upon them that they are important, but they ultimately make the decision.

I had to make the decision myself. I knew what I was being told or taught. I was in church too. You get messages from lots of things. Maybe I'd keep them involved in a lot of religious things too. I don't know. I don't know what would help children nowadays. Lord help them!

I would teach kids of different sexes in another way. Boys are so nasty; they can't help it. Honestly, I feel that way. They're not all that way, but I know initially they have to be. I feel like the younger boys are and the older ones are just curious. I would tell them I understand and respect their curiosities, *but* it's still not something to tamper with. Sex is not for kids. I don't know. I just hope we would always be open. I'd hate to scare them off. But I'm sure I'd be the type that would stress caution to them enough where they probably wouldn't come to me right away. That's unfortunate. I would really love it if we had open communication, and I would know what they were considering.

My message to my daughter or son would probably be, *"People don't pay much respect and value to sex, what it means or their bodies after sex occurs. Since you never know whose going to be number one, value and respect keeps you safest."* You don't see it when you're young. You're just out having a good time. And I've observed it's easier for you to have sex. I think you place less value on yourself if sex comes easily to you or if you don't think of yourself or your sexuality as valuable.

Heather

When I have kids, I would be honest with them and upfront. At the same time, I'd try to shelter them. I don't know. That's a tough one. I would be honest at the right age. If they asked me a question, depending on how old they are, I would answer. If my little kid asked me the name of something, I'd tell them. If they asked where babies came from, I'd tell them they come from the love between a man and a woman. I wouldn't tell them exactly. If I had a boy and a girl who were the same age, there wouldn't be a difference between what I'd tell one or the other.

Katherine

If I had kids, I would like to talk to them about sexuality. I wouldn't just buy a book like my Mom. I guess my question is, *"What is the appropriate age?"* You don't want to put ideas in their head like society. I wouldn't want my kid to learn about it in the street like I did. Originally, I would want to treat

> my son and daughter the same. But seeing how guys are so different, I don't know if I'd want my husband to talk with them with me present or separately. I don't want to treat them differently, but it might happen. I still feel I'm naïve on sexual content, and I'm in my 30s.

The Cole family's responses are very interesting when you compare them to the answers they gave in previous chapters. Mrs. Cole indicates she was open to talk to her daughters and make educational books available to them. Yet in Chapter 2, Emily says she and her sisters had no reference in the home for sexuality. Heather said the message she received from her parents was "sex is bad." Katherine is the only person who mentioned the sex education book to which Mrs. Cole refers.

Mr. Cole stated he did not have anything to teach his girls, but he was more forthcoming than his wife. In Chapter 2, Katherine said she went to her father for help with a sexual education test in the 11th grade when her mother was unable to answer her questions. While the physiology and anatomy of a girl's growing body may be better explained by a knowledgeable woman, young girls also benefit from a father or male role model's guidance in other areas of sexuality, such as the stages a boy goes through as his body matures. Children and teenagers of both sexes benefit from learning about each other.

Katherine asked an invaluable question, "What is the appropriate age to start discussing sexuality with a child?" Many people debate as to what the "right" age is. In Chapter 3, it was stated that kids start exploring their bodies as early as age three or four. Medical doctors at the Mayo Foundation for Education and Research also say children between the ages of five and seven, start asking more detailed questions about sexuality and may pick up the wrong information from friends.[8] So it is best to start educating them as soon as possible.

Some people think a six year-old is too young to be taught anything about sexuality. It is necessary for children to be taught the correct function of their body parts and sexual organs, the right to have their personal boundaries respected and how to voice their comfort or discomfort in any situation. They are entitled to know the truth about anything they inquire about. Using age-appropriate language, suitable to their level of comprehension, can best accomplish this.

Establishing open and honest communication is vital to strengthening our children and families. *"Not telling a child exactly"* where babies come from or that *"they come from the love between a man and a woman,"* as Heather mentioned, is too vague and unclear. Babies can be born to adults who do not love each other at all. Sometimes babies are born as a result of non-consensual sex. Taking the biological view, babies are produced from sexual intercourse between a man and woman. If love is involved, it is a blessing. Without honesty, we place communication barriers between parents and children.

We further handicap our children and teenagers when we focus only on the possible consequences of them physically expressing their sexuality. In reality, many teens and adults do have sex before they are married. In 1998, the Henry J. Kaiser Family Foundation and teen magazine, *YM*, conducted a national survey with 650 teenagers about their sexual experiences. Their results showed that 31% of teens ages 13 to 18 had sexual intercouse.[9] The Center of Disease Control reported in 1999 that 49.9 percent of high school students had sexual intercourse.[10]

Conflicting messages make it hard for boys and girls to see each other as equals and value their differences. Girls have just as many sexual curiosities as boys do. However, boys are conditioned to be vocal about their curiosities while girls are taught to suppress them. *"Boys are just nasty; they can't help it,"* as expressed by Emily, reflects how American culture is encouraged to view boys. It is a stereotype implied through false expectations, like expecting girls to remain virgins while boys are encouraged to be sexually experienced before marriage. With this dangerous conditioning, we help create an environment where young boys could unknowingly be perpetrators of sexual violence if we do not teach them to respect the boundaries and bodies of other people and themselves.

WALKER FAMILY

Mrs. Walker

I read books on their level, even if they were in elementary school. Now you have a large selection of books for adults that you can get to show children. If my children came and asked me where a baby came from, I made sure I had that book, *Mom, Where Do Babies Come From?* I remember that book. I would start from page one and go all the way to the end when the mother was ready to have the baby. I would explain every step to them. But I would use the words they could understand and words they could grow with. I didn't want them to think there was anything degrading about sex.

I never ever in my life used the "birds and bees," because I was so sick of it. Every time we asked questions when we were young; that's all we were told. So I would never use that. I would use a man and a woman, or a boy and a girl, or either just a male and a female. I let them know it was two humans and it had nothing to do with animals, even though they do the same thing.

To be very honest with you, I can't remember everything. But if any of my kids ever came and asked me anything pertaining to sex, I did answer. I tried to answer them to the best of my ability at that time with whatever I knew. If I didn't know, I would go out and try to find an answer for them. But if I'm not mistaken, I believe I told them both the same thing. I felt it was very important for Paul not to just understand himself, but also to understand a woman. The same thing applies to Patricia. I felt like we are looking at two humans, and they just happen to be of a different sex. I think for one sex to know about the other is just as important as them knowing about himself or herself.

Paul

I'm just going to be honest with my daughters. If you try to sugarcoat and hide stuff, it makes it worse. So the best way to tackle it is to be honest. Just sit them down and talk to them. That's the best way. There'd be no difference if I had a boy. It's the same. Females have to respect themselves. But a male has to respect himself too. I know I'm not having anymore kids in the future.

Patricia

Well, right now, I started teaching my son. At four, he knows all his body parts. He knows that nobody touches his "pee pee" or his bottom. If they do, he tells Mommy, and Mommy is going to whoop the people who touch him. From there on up, I think some things are natural or a learned behavior as far as "boys like girls." I guess you would have to eventually have that talk, but I think that's kind of natural. I guess you start with that, *"You're supposed to like girls. You don't go around touching girls here or there; that's inappropriate."* I guess I'd teach him about respecting his own body, not sleeping around, and about all the things going on in the world. He'd know the same basics I was taught, *"You want to wait. You want to care about the other person."* I think I would have to take another step with him because males are more so the aggressor in sexual situations. So I guess I would have to teach him, *"Don't be out here playin' with these little girls' feelings. Don't be touchin' all on them and sleepin' with 'em,"* and stuff like that.

If I had a girl, I think my teaching would be along the same lines. There might be a slight difference. The basics of dating would be the same. The only difference teaching the girl would be, *"You could get pregnant. If you get pregnant this baby is yours. He can walk away."* I think that would be the only difference with a girl. I would teach my son the same thing, hoping that he would respect himself and any woman he sleeps with. But again he still has that choice of walking away. So I guess it would be kind of different.

When asked about her family upbringing in Chapter 2, Mrs. Walker stated she went through difficulties as a child due to the lack of education she received about sexuality. She attempted to make up for that by being available to her children so they could ask her anything they wanted. Paul, however, does not follow his mother's example. Based on his answers, he does not give evidence that he educates his daughter about sexuality. Paul's oldest daughter is a preteen—an age where sexuality information is vital. She could benefit by learning from her father and hearing his perspective. Perhaps Paul leaves the majority of the education to his daughter's mother. Whether the biological parents are together or not, children benefit from both parents educating them on sexuality, especially when parents and guardians can give correct and complete information from their honest perspectives.

Patricia has started teaching her son about sexuality by focusing on his body parts. She even let him know that no one is supposed to touch his penis or bottom, which is commendable. Where she goes from here could be a cause for concern. Telling our children what they are "supposed to do" can be tricky. *"You are supposed to like girls,"* is what Patricia intends to tell her son as part of his sexuality education. He will most likely be attracted to girls though there is still much debate regarding what is learned behavior versus natural behavior. Still, most boys will have an attraction to girls while a small percentage will have an attraction to other boys. Data from a 2002 study by the National Center for Health Statistics showed that less than 1% of boys, ages 15 to 19, had a same sex partner in the previous year.[11] (It is important to note this statistic does not show the percentage of boys who admit an *attraction* to other boys. Males can be attracted to other males without engaging in sexual behavior.)

Patricia will also tell her son not to play with "little girls' feelings" and not to "touch and sleep with them." These statements may not be enough to tell a growing boy when many popular socio-cultural institutions in this country tell him it is okay to use women and have as many sexual partners as he pleases. Most children and adolescents will develop natural sexual desires. Dr. Donna Gaffney emphasizes the following facts referring to males, *"Boys and young men learn about sexual arousal and responsiveness at a young age. They can visually recognize sexual arousal. They are aware of the feelings in their bodies and how they can increase pleasurable sensations."*[12] If we do not want our boys *playing with girls' feelings*, we must teach them how their bodies function, especially their physiological sexual response. Then, it is essential for knowledgeable male role models to educate boys on how to express their sexual desires responsibly. It is just as important for girls to be taught the same. Training young boys to respect a girl's body, space and her right to say no to unwanted sexual comments and advances will have a remarkable impact on the mental, emotional, physical and spiritual health of our families and communities.

RYAN FAMILY

Mrs. Ryan

I did teach my boys—that's for certain. I told them there was really nothing dirty about sex, and it's clean. But it's nothing to play with, because you can bring kids into the world. Then you have to be responsible. At the same time, I knew that I couldn't be with my kids every second of the day to see what they were doing no more than my mom was with us. I figured I could tell them better because of some things I experienced when I started having kids. I'm not saying to go out there and have sex. Just make sure you are protected because it's not a game. If I had girls, I think I would have told them the same thing I told the boys. I may have to repeat it more. It just depends. In some ways, girls could be a little different. I know boys.

Mr. Ryan

I tried to explain to them, *"If you're gonna do it, use protection."* With boys you are more lenient. I didn't encourage them to have sex. I guess I started talking to them when an incident happened with my neighbor's daughter. One of my sons was lying on top of the girl, saying it was his brother's fault. He was seven or eight. If I had raised my daughter [from a previous relationship], I would have been stricter. I tried to tell my daughter not to act wild.

<u>Otis</u>

I started telling my kids to be conscious of what can happen if you ponder that aspect of life too soon. My son and I started talking in eighth grade. I talked with him regarding the attention well-developed female students his age were getting. I know from TV and the news, kids are impregnating each other at age 13. I told him it was best to wait until his late junior year in high school to have sex.

My wife talked to our daughter. I added on to that. We see the news on TV about girls being kidnapped and raped. When my son's guy friends call or come to the door, my daughter is the first one there. I see it. I know why she's rushing to the door. I know it's the sexuality kickin' in. She knows what I'm talking about when I bring it to her attention.

The more skin females show, the more males are going to be aroused. My daughter wants to imitate the style she sees on TV somewhat. The low cut shirts, pants with your butt hanging out, shirts with the arms and shoulders out with the lace on the side, little tank tops or belly button shirts showing your navel are things we don't approve of.

There wasn't a big difference between what we told them because one is a boy and the other is a girl. Not having sex or not pondering the image the TV gives off is what I say to both of them. My son is older, so that's the difference. I told him dating should wait until late junior year because his grades shouldn't suffer in his senior year. That year is easy. I didn't say, *"Go out and have sex."* If he waited until his graduation night, I'd be happy for him. By his senior year, he should be able to maintain his grades and a girlfriend.

For my daughter, it wouldn't be her senior year. I'd tell her to wait at least until after two years of college—age 23 or 24. Maybe earlier if she does well in high school. The mind has to be ready. If she got pregnant without the financial backing, she's slowing herself down. I'd feel bad if someone had to wait between high school and age 24 if they really wanted to have sex. But the risk is pregnancy. At her age, you'd have to put them on something [birth control] which sends a message right there. I don't want to see her pregnant until 24 or 25. I wouldn't be mad if it happened earlier, if she was married and had a man to support her. Seeing what I went through, having my first kid at 19, I felt like I could've lived a lot more.

The Ryans are different from the other families in that with the exception of Mrs. Ryan, it is an all male household. Mr. and Mrs. Ryan appear to have a more lenient attitude about sex with their sons than other members of the Peterson family. It is almost as if they expected them to have sex at an early age. There is no mention of telling their sons to wait until they were married. The only topic mentioned with concern is a fear that their sons would have gotten someone pregnant before they were ready. Ironically, Otis became a father at the age of 19.

Otis' double standard in raising his son and daughter is obvious. His son can start dating late in his junior year of high school, but he wants his daughter to wait until she is a junior in college because of his fear of her becoming pregnant. Otis does not want to put his daughter on birth control if she wants to have sex because he fears she will look at it as permission to have sex. Parents and guardians do not always understand that a teenager will have sex regardless of whether or not they are on birth control. Otis is projecting his fears onto his daughter, yet he would be okay if his son had sex on the night of his high school graduation. He did not voice any concern about his son getting someone pregnant. Sending biased messages in favor of boys to children of both genders within the same household can result in girls feeling less valued than boys, depending on how the messages are digested.

While Otis did tune into the sexual images and messages portrayed on television, it often is not enough. We need to teach our sons and daughters responsibility. The double standards they see within their own households are the double standards they will use when they date and raise children of their own. Otis may not have said, "*Go out and have sex,*" but as his children get older, the message will be clear, whether verbalized or not: *If you are a boy, it's okay to have sex. If you are a girl, you shouldn't have sex until you are 23, and can take care of yourself because, if you get pregnant, a guy doesn't have to be there.*

Otis' cousin, Patricia, expressed a similar message earlier. If she had a daughter, she would tell her that having a baby would be her responsibility because the guy can walk away. These fear-based messages and unhealthy stereotypes have our children attempting to live up to an unrealistic standard that many adults have not achieved or maintained. Teenage boys and girls are having sex with each other. To assume it would not be your daughter or son is a mistake too many parents make.

DAVID PETERSON

Mr. Peterson

My oldest daughter is 13. My son is 10. My youngest daughter is seven. I can't say what we have done as parents to educate our kids about sexuality, but I will say what I believe in doing. I believe in being honest with my kids. I am honest with my kids. To me, that's the best way. My kids have asked me questions before. I've educated my son on his body parts. At age seven I told him, *"When you see this thing in your hand and it's a stiff rod that means you are supposed to do something with it"* [laughter]. If the girls wanted to know something sexual, I told them, *"It's best to deal with your mother."* Sometimes they didn't want to deal with their mother, so I'd tell them the best of what I knew. They never asked me questions about how people get pregnant or things like that.

There is a little difference between my daughters and son, but not much. The reason is because my son is a male like I am. I need to tell him certain things. I

71

guess you could say females don't need to know about that stuff. For example, I would tell my son, *"You may get married. Don't you ever go and put your hands on another woman."* I would also tell him, *"Son, if you are single, go out there and tear them all up!"* On the other hand, I would tell my oldest daughter, *"Don't let none of them n*ggas get they hands on you"* [laughter]. That means don't go out and have no sex unless you're married. That's the same message to my son also. If my daughter was to go out and get pregnant, I'd tell her, *"Make sure you keep the n*gga intact."* If my son was to go out and get a woman pregnant, I'd tell him, *"Make sure you take care of what you did."*

Mr. Peterson contradicted himself while answering this question, so it is a challenge to discern which statement reflects his true feelings. For example, when his son was seven, Mr. Peterson told him he's supposed to use his penis when it's erect. Even though Mr. Peterson was laughing when he said this, I believe there was some truth to his statement. Whether or not he was referring to masturbation is unclear. If his son is single, he'd encourage him to sleep with as many women as possible. Yet his daughters are instructed not to allow anyone to touch them. The language that Mr. Peterson uses, *"Son, if you are single, go out there and tear them all up,"* sexually objectifies women.

Later on, Mr. Peterson said he would tell his son and daughters to wait until marriage for sex. Which is the truth? If Mr. Peterson's "tear women up" advice to his son reflects his true beliefs, it is an example of messages that encourage men to aggressively pursue women for sexual gratification, regardless of a woman's feelings. These messages lay the foundation for a society that encourages and supports a culture filled with sexual violence. Destructive messages such as these must be challenged. Double standards and gender inequality regarding raising our children must come to an end if we want children within our families to be safe. Too many parents do not realize the importance of discussing sexual abuse with their children as part of their sexuality education talks.

Chapter 5

What do we know about sexual abuse?

When asked what they taught their children about sexuality, Otis Ryan and Patricia Walker were the only members of the Peterson family who mentioned sexual abuse and molestation. Otis and his wife knew about teenage girls being kidnapped and raped. Patricia told her son no one is supposed to touch his "pee-pee" or bottom. If someone did, he was instructed and expected to tell his mother.

While raising their children, none of the Peterson siblings nor their spouses mentioned sexual abuse to their children. That information was not passed down to them from Mama and Papa Peterson. This is not surprising given the time period in which the Petersons grew up. So the next logical question to ask was if anyone remembered any incidents of sexual abuse, whether or not they personally knew the people involved. Seven out of twelve adults in the Peterson family remembered at least one specific sexual abuse incident of which they were aware. Yet, no one in the previous chapter, besides Otis and Patricia, thought of preparing their children for this possibility.

Discussing sexuality is limited when it focuses only on teenage pregnancy and sexually transmitted diseases.

Did your parents or any adults talk to you about what you should do if someone touched you inappropriately as a child?

Do you know of any past or current incidents of child sexual abuse in general?

COLE FAMLY

Mrs. Cole

I don't know of sexual abuse situations with my friends or co-workers. I've had some cousins who I thought were sexually abused. No one ever talked about child sexual abuse. I don't think it was talked about in school or church either. But you sort of know that's wrong. It's almost like an instinct. You know there are certain places that other people are not supposed to touch unless it's your mother giving you a bath. It just shouldn't happen. If it does, you need to tell somebody else about it. You go to your parents or you go to a teacher. Nobody talked to me. If someone touched me in certain places, I would have felt and known it was not the right thing.

Mr. Cole

I'm sure the topic came up about adults not touching you sexually, but I can't remember. I could talk to my father or uncle. I don't remember them or my mother saying anything. I'm not saying it didn't happen to someone else; I just don't remember. Back in those days I don't think it was as prevalent as it is now. Things have evolved since then. There are so many predators out there. At least the convicted ones are supposed to be registered in certain states; that helps. Some families are so broken up and that's not good. Too many different people are coming in their homes.

There was something on TV last week. One little boy was sexually abused by a registered predator here in Memphis. He was nine or ten years old. Then a case involving a priest got overturned. He had done three different things. One of the charges against him was exposure or fondling a little boy. The parents were outraged that the courts overturned the case. The priest was a predator. Since he only showed himself to kids, he got less time for it. The parents are going to appeal it.

Emily

Well, you always hear about sex crimes in the news, such as rape. The word rape itself was always prevalent. You would hear it and know that it existed. The only time it came up close and personal to me was when I was working my first job.

When I was still here in Memphis, one of the first jobs I had after I got out of school was working with developmentally delayed ladies. They would go home on the weekends. One lady consistently came back bruised up with hickies on her chest. The sad thing about it was we were speculating the father was involved. It wasn't my job to handle it, but we knew it was him. In her case, she could not speak; she could only use sign language. Even she knew or appeared to not want to say who did what. What do you say? She was pretty young, maybe 20. I always thought that was sad.

I worked for Big Brothers Big Sisters one time. I was responsible for connecting the big brothers and sisters with the children. We had to look out for pedophiles. I asked myself, *"Were they weird?"* We interviewed volunteers by doing a home study. We'd go over to their house and look around for the "right" trigger things. If you had a bad vibe or when they were around the child and you didn't get a good feeling, we were told to go by your instinct. I felt very uncomfortable doing that. More so because I was afraid of getting the instinct that told me the potential big brother or sister was a pedophile. I never had the experience, but the organization made us very aware of it. Pedophiles would be drawn to our kind of organization.

Even in terms of Michael Jackson, the boy they have accusing him felt like Michael was his friend. In this case, it's sticky because there are others who feel the mom prodded the child to say things that might not be true. I'm not certain if the child is being prodded to say it. I think Michael is weird, but I always thought he was asexual. I didn't think he was having sex with anyone. But it bothers me to think that he is with young boys. That really bugs me. He's sick, if that is the case. I wanted to marry him when I was six. I look at him now and I think, *"Eww! What have you become?"* I didn't think anything was wrong with him. I just thought he had a self-hatred or a hatred of being Black or something of that nature. I always thought that was the reason for changing the nose, coloring and everything else he's done to himself. But this is ugly to me. If this is something he's been hiding around, I can't believe that's the first child this has happened to.

I'm sure my parents told me what to do if someone touched me the wrong way. We didn't talk about it a lot, but I'm sure they always said it was a "no-no." You knew it was a "no-no." I mean you just knew it was bad. I hear it more now. As a little kid I heard it but not a lot. I'm sure my mom told me. No one specifically told me what to do if something like that happened, but you knew you should tell Mommy. All I remember is my parents saying, *"Nobody is supposed to do that, you know. Let us know if they do."*

Heather

I'd have to say no. I don't remember my parents talking to me about grown ups trying to take advantage of me as a kid. Teachers in school may have brought it up. It seemed like at that age things like that were done, but not as often as they are now.

There was an incident with a Catholic priest here. I absolutely adored him. Katherine and I would go to mass at church when he would do it. Then one day on the news, they said he was sent back to his hometown because of molesting a boy in 1978. It broke my trust with the priest and the Catholic religion.

Katherine

The talks back when I was a kid were more so along the lines of, *"Don't talk to strangers."* No one said, *"Don't let people touch you."* My mom may have talked about sexual molestation once or it might have been discussed at school.

I'm a social worker. We had to take a mandated child sexual abuse class for my job. The class was boring and awful because my group knew everything. What I found ridiculous was that some people had no clue! Unfortunately, most of them were Black. The people at my table were flabbergasted that other people didn't know how much kids are sexually abused. How could you not know? This class was for people who worked with children.

My co-workers and I speculate something is going on with a couple of students. One is a nine year-old girl. We know something happened to an 11th grader, but she was abused in the eighth grade. We found out from the friends she hung around. The friends were doing drugs and she would ask them *"what if"* questions as if she were talking about someone else. Another incident involved my friend's husband. His sister accused their brother of molesting her and another sister. Their mom sent him to Montana to live with his father. Now everyone thinks it was actually the stepfather who molested them. The brother said something that led us to believe he was covering for someone else—maybe a friend.

Mrs. Cole *assumes* she would have known it was not right for an adult to sexually touch her as a child. Many children do not know. They trust adults, especially those who are supposed to protect them. If a child is conditioned by an abuser that sexual molestation is normal, the child has no way of knowing otherwise until (s)he is exposed to external messages elsewhere. The result is a child who feels shame because (s)he was manipulated and forced to engage in a behavior that is against the law and socially unacceptable. What "instinct" is in place that alerts a child to "know" there are places certain people are not supposed to touch?

Emily believes her parents had a talk with her, while Heather and Katherine clearly state that no one had talked with them about sexual abuse. By the time Katherine was in school, the standard message was

"Don't Talk To Strangers." Yet this message does nothing to address the prevalence of abuse that occurs most often. According to the United States Department of Justice, family members and acquaintances account for 93% of sexual assaults against people under age 18.[13]

Attention must also be given to Heather's broken trust in the Catholic religion. Any adult can harm a child regardless of his/her position in a religious community or professional setting. In addition to Catholic priests sexually abusing children, there are also documented cases of ministers convicted of sexually abusing children in their congregation and their own biological children. On October 21, 2004, the *Oprah Winfrey Show* featured three adult sisters who were raped by their minister father from the time they were children throughout their adolescence. It may be hard for some people to accept, but ministers and priests are not immune to the programming and conditioning that makes sexual abuse so prevalent within our society.

Sexual arousal exists within all of us, but some spiritual leaders do not have a healthy, appropriate outlet to channel it. When any religion describes sexual arousal as something unnatural or unclean, this can cause tension for those people who want to engage in appropriate, healthy sexual behavior. The previous statements do not condone or defend religious and spiritual leaders for their crimes and violations against children and teenagers. However, it is important to recognize the additional sexual conflicts and issues some of them wrestle with in their environment if we want to effectively end this problem. There are also cases of nuns sexually abusing and molesting girls.[14] We must use caution and refrain from letting the crimes of some spiritual and religious leaders cause us to doubt our own spiritual values and beliefs.

WALKER FAMILY

Mrs. Walker

No one said anything to me about adults touching or trying to feel you up. Back then, I don't think we had to worry about that. A lot of things could have been taking place, but I wasn't aware or exposed to certain things. I never had people grabbing or touching me inappropriately. I never went through that. When I became a teenager, you started hearing men in their cars whistle at you while you were walking. That's basically it.

I can remember one incident a co-worker told me about on a past job. If I'm not mistaken, I was a temp sent on this particular assignment. One lady would talk about her son all the time and how he would climb into bed with her. I can't remember the exact words she used because it's been a while, but it sounded like very *very* explicit sex. I know he was between the age of six or seven. Every evening, she said, he'd have to come and rub in between her thighs and stuff like that. He would get an erection. It was, in other words a "no no." She went way across the line. I felt she was almost using her own son. It could've gone even further than what she told us. Later, I found out she was a nympho, where she'd leave at lunch time to go and get sex. The boss was aware of this. I think she pulled her son into this. I know he would sleep with her. Everything that a man did to her, I think her son pretty much did the same thing. She would talk about it very openly because she saw nothing wrong with it.

Paul

I think we read about adults trying to touch kids in school or something like that. Outside of school, I didn't hear about stuff like that. I haven't heard of anything like that today.

Patricia

I don't recall anyone talking to me about adults touching kids sexually. The only incidents I know about are things I see on TV. I hear of stuff in the media all the time. I've never known of anything personally. That was never brought up to me as a child. My mother never said, *"If this or that happens, then you need to come to me."* A lot of things my mother will tell me today because she never thought about it in the past. She didn't know. I guess everybody lives in an *"it won't happen to me"* world. It never happened to me or to anyone that was close to me or around me.

Given Mrs. Walker's earlier responses, it is no surprise that she knew nothing about child sexual abuse. Mrs. Walker's account of a former co-worker having a sexual relationship with her son is a type of abuse many people in society do not hear about. We are rarely informed of instances involving a mother sexually abusing her children. Adult women abuse children too, though their numbers are low in comparison to men. In 2000, the Center for Sex Offender Management highlighted statistics from the FBI and Association for the Treatment of Sexual Abusers, stating that females were 8% of all rape and sexual assault arrests for 1997 and other studies showed they committed approximately 20% of sex offenses against children.[15]

RYAN FAMILY

Mrs. Ryan

I don't remember Mama saying, *"Don't let the men..."* For me, it would go back to when Mama would say, *"Keep your dress down. Don't let the boys pat or feel on you because it's just gonna lead to something else."* She meant any part of your body.

Before I was married, we would go to parties. I questioned the style of dancing. I would wonder, *"Is this person just feeling on me or is this just a normal dance?"* But nobody wants to be touched by an adult because it doesn't make you feel good. It's different from taking someone by their hand or brushing by somebody while you are walking. As I grew older, *then* I realized adults shouldn't do this.

I think I've heard of sexual abuse incidents from friends when they were young. They could've been talking about what happened to them or someone else. A lot of people don't use names.

Mr. Ryan

No, my mom didn't talk to me about adults touching me. Back then, it wasn't as bad as it is now. If it happened, it was very few people. I was raised in a white neighborhood. I've never witnessed women touching kids. I didn't hear about it until I went into the service. Now I only hear about sexual abuse in the news.

Otis

I don't remember anyone telling me to watch out for adults as a kid. I'm sure it came up at school, but I don't remember when. I experienced sexual things on and off, but I wasn't doing enough where someone said something to me.

I can recall of a teacher and student incident. The female teacher initiated sexual contact with a male student. I think he was 16. She was well in her late 20s. There are a lot of other ones too. In the news, they said a guy spent the night at his friend's house. At night, he took their little girl from the house out into an area and tried to rape her. Then he hit her on the head with a brick and killed her. He's on trial now.

Mr. Ryan's statements seem to say that he didn't hear a lot about child sexual abuse because he grew up in a white neighborhood. Perhaps he did not hear about abuse because as a Black child growing up in the 1940s and 1950s, it was unlikely that white peers would interact with him. The occurrence of intra-cultural sexual abuse exists in all ethnic groups in the United States. In other words, when it comes to race and ethnicity, no one group of people is safer than the other.

Mrs. Ryan's instructions from her mother also reflect the time period of the mid 1940s throughout the 1950s. Giving a girl an instruction to "keep your dress down," unfairly puts the responsibility of a boy's sexual desire on her. Today, we all should know that the way a girl sits or the clothes she wears will not stop someone from attempting to sexually molest or abuse her. The guidance Mrs. Ryan's mother gave her is a common thought pattern that has trickled down into the present. It puts the responsibility of how men physically view and approach women squarely on the shoulders of women.

Otis' recollection of a female teacher having a sexual relationship with a male student is often given a different spin in the media than a male teacher having sex with a female student. The older female is usually portrayed as a sex-crazed woman who found passion with a boy younger than herself. Many of these stories are portrayed in a more romantic way suggesting and encouraging that younger men have sexual fantasies of being seduced by older women. In this patriarchal society, where most sexuality images cater to men, most people find it difficult to accept that when a woman sexually abuses or molests a boy, it can be just as traumatic as a girl being abused by a man.

DAVID PETERSON

Mr. Peterson

Nobody ever warned me about anything as a little kid. I made myself aware, 'cause I knew one damn thing, I ain't no fuckin' faggot! What I mean by "I ain't no damn faggot" is I know a man should not be with a man. A woman should not be with a woman.

That's what I believe. A man should be with a woman.

If I had to be sexually abused, I would love for the woman to touch me, 'cause if a man ever would've touched me, I would have killed him. I can't say that I was abused. I only hear about sexual abuse on the news; that's about it.

Mr. Peterson is a wonderful example of how a man can equate sexual abuse by a woman with seduction. Contrary to popular myth, little boys do not necessarily enjoy being sexually abused, whether the abuser is a man or a woman. It is also evident here that Mr. Peterson is uncomfortable with homosexuality and is sensitive to being labeled as such. He adamantly proclaims he is heterosexual, even though his sexual orientation was never questioned.

It is not surprising that Mr. Peterson believes he would have killed his abuser. Many men have the illusion that as a child they could have possessed the strength to physically overpower an abusive adult. A child who is sexually abused by someone in the family would most likely feel a high degree of powerlessness and betrayal, accompanied by an intense feeling of guilt and shame. A male teenager, on the other hand, may tend to believe that he, like Mr. Peterson, could successfully challenge a sexual assault.

Chapter 6

That Dirty Word—Incest

Incest is sexual contact between people who are so closely related that legal marriage between them would not be permitted. An example would be a sister and brother, parent and child, first cousins or aunt and niece or nephew. Sexual contact between a stepfather and stepdaughter also qualifies. Incestuous abuse occurs when a family member sexually abuses another family member. In cases of child sexual abuse, incest usually happens when an adult or older family member takes advantage of a child or teenager. Many experts consider incest the most damaging form of sexual abuse because individuals who children trust to protect them are the violators.

The U.S. Department of Justice's, Sexual Assault of Young Children Report, cited incest as the most common form of sexual abuse for children under the age of six.[16] It is important to note that these statistics are based on *reported* incidents to law enforcement agencies. Diana Russell's groundbreaking book, *The Secret Trauma*, explored incest in the lives of girls and women. In her study, 648 female participants out of 930 disclosed being victims of child sexual abuse. Only 30 of those incidents were reported to authorities. Four of those cases were incestuous abuse.[17] It is well known among therapists and counselors working with survivors of sexual abuse, that incest is the least likely form of sexual abuse reported. For this reason, many believe incest is the most prevalent form of child sexual abuse.

Members of the Peterson family were asked if they were aware of how widespread incest is and if they were aware of the possibility of it happening in their own backyard. Most parents and guardians warn their children to be aware of strangers. Some parents go a step further by encouraging their children to let them know if anyone tries to sexually violate them. In spite of these efforts, the numbers of people who are both aware and vocal about such individuals in their own families are few. After reflecting on sexuality within the context of their upbringing and examining society, it was time to see how much the Petersons knew about sexual abuse in their own family.

Did you know that incest is one of the most common forms of child sexual abuse?

Have you heard of child sexual abuse happening within your family?

COLE FAMILY

<u>Mrs. Cole</u>

When I first heard about incest as an adult, I thought it was insane. I may have been in my 30s. I just couldn't believe it. I didn't know about it as a teenager. I hadn't heard anything about it in my 20s. But now people are growing more and more evil. You hear more about it. I had to figure out and learn that word *incest*.

The person who I know was molested was a teenager. I don't know if my cousin was molested when she was younger. This happened within the family. I guess her family knew after she got pregnant. Her stepfather did it. She had the child and everything. I found out when I was a teenager. No actions were taken. They lived together as one happy family. Back then, you really couldn't make a big deal of it. When everything is so *hush-hush,* things aren't talked about. The only thing you could do was keep it quiet.

<u>Mr. Cole</u>

Oh my goodness! I didn't know so much sex abuse occurred in families. Wow. That's sad; it really is. Over the last 20-40 years, I'm sure society has changed. Maybe now it's just coming out. More divorces are happening now. Those live-in boyfriends and steps have no feelings for these kids like a parent should.

I can't remember anyone in my family saying anything about someone being abused. I could probably go out and ask somebody now if it happened. I don't know what they would say. Back in those days, nobody told you things like that. I can't remember anything happening in the neighborhood either. I lived in a Black and white community at that time and this didn't happen. If it did, it was kept quiet and the kids didn't know about it. I think I would've heard about a kid being abused through the grapevine, if it happened. Somebody would've said something.

<u>Emily</u>

I did not know a lot of abuse occurs in the family, but I would believe it. You have to be able to get close to individuals in order to get to a point to where you can abuse them. It doesn't surprise me. You always see stuff on TV with parents and children abusing! I would hear things. They used to say Elvis' [Rock and Roll singer Elvis Presley] mom was weird, and that he slept with her longer than necessary. Remember the Menendez boys who killed their parents in California a few years back? They said that their parents had abused them and used that for their defense. Those boys are in jail—never to get out. So yeah, I would believe that. But it doesn't have to be that way.

It'd be wrong to say I *know* of anything that happened in my family. This had not ever been an issue to me before. It's not fair, because this was something my sister and I discussed directly, which related to our cousin's issues. One cousin made a very inflammatory remark recently towards an uncle. It bothered me to hear it because I never envisioned that particular uncle going there. It wasn't clear to me what happened. I'm pressed for saying what's what. I'm not certain what is considered abuse or molestation. The same uncle is two years older than me. He and I used to play games. I don't recall of anything like that. We played doctor, but nothing felt bad or was an incident to go home and cry to

Mommy about. *"You've got a pee pee. I've got a pee pee,"* is as much as I can recall. But I'm bothered by what my cousin said, and I don't like hearsay.

I'm not saying it's impossible. What I heard just came up. I felt like more needed to be said. I don't think my cousin completely spelled it out to my sister either as far as I'm concerned. When she and I talked further, I thought, *"Is all this because of the Michael Jackson stuff coming up? Is he hearing this stuff in the news and just now thinking what occurred is bad? Or did he always know it?"*

In addition to the uncle, the cousin also brought up his sibling's name. That bothers me now because I think of the fact that those particular men are grown and have children. That's why I hope, *"Please let this be a misunderstanding."* But I don't see how you can misunderstand that. He sounded vehemently angry about it. It just breaks my heart. I've never felt anything like that. That's why I can say I can't acknowledge anything in my nature that even comes close to that. Up until then, I had never heard any family-related incident. That's the honest truth. I have to tell you what I *heard* even though I feel funny discussing it. I've seen other little kids playing in the way I mentioned earlier. I wasn't involved. They were cousins but I don't see that as abuse. I did not catch them engaging in an *act*. I see that as little kids playing.

Heather

I didn't know that. I guess it doesn't surprise me. You hear about incidents on the news. It's so nasty and really bothers me. I guess it does kinda surprise me. There's a lot of stuff I'm unaware of. I don't know about anything like that happening in my family. There's other shit but nothing like that.

Katherine
Yes, I know all about incest. It blows my mind
that some people think it's normal! Some boyfriend
of my aunt molested my two cousins [girls] on my
dad's side. The allegations were that he definitely
molested one of them. It happened when I was little
or before I was born. I don't know what happened to
the boyfriend. One of my cousins is still messed up to
this day.

Most adults of Mr. and Mrs. Cole's generation were unaware of
the prevalence of incestuous abuse. Mrs. Cole had not heard of the
word "incest" until she was in her 30s, even though she knew her
cousin had a child by her stepfather. Katherine's cousins, who were
molested by an aunt's boyfriend, would qualify as incest only if the
boyfriend was their stepfather.

Emily's reluctant disclosure of the "rumor" she "heard" regarding
her cousin is very disturbing to her. She has been exposed to sexual
abuse in a few work settings. It is surprising then, that she doubts and
questions the validity of her cousin's accusations. She is a perfect
example of the difficulty many people experience when confronted
with the possibility that someone you love and respect within your
family is a perpetrator of child sexual abuse or in a simple,
frightening word—incest.

WALKER FAMILY

<u>Mrs. Walker</u>

Well, I didn't know a lot of abuse was in the family, but I could believe that now. It surprises me none whatsoever. I think for a long time everything was swept under the carpet. So I believe a lot of things took place years and years ago but were never talked about. I think a child really believes and puts trust in an adult or in their parents or older brother or sister. A lot of things a child may have went along with; they might not have known was wrong at that particular time.

For example, if while growing up as a little girl, my father told me to do certain things, I would not have thought nothing of it. I would have done what my father asked me to do because I felt like he was right. In other words, when you are a child, you really don't have a concept of certain things unless you have parents that are teaching you at a very, very young age. I think it's talked about more now. Back in the past, I would say nothing was talked about. I believe a whole lot of incest went on in the past. I really do. I think a lot of it has an effect on our males and females even today. I think a lot of our males were sexually molested more than we realize. We tend to think females, but I think a lot of males have been sexually abused too.

The ones that I knew about in my family were adults. I couldn't even say they were abusing each other. I think they indulged in it very freely and felt like there was nothing wrong with that.

<u>Paul</u>

Yeah, I'm surprised because incest ain't something you hear about. So if you don't hear or talk about it, then you don't really trip off of it. Then if somebody brings it up, you'll think, *"Aw, that didn't happen!"* Or you'll just keep on brushing it off. I don't know of anything in my family, on either side.

Patricia

Yeah, I had heard abuse goes down in the family. It could be uncles, cousins, brothers—it doesn't matter. I was surprised. When I was a kid, if my mother said, *"I have to go to work and you have to go with your uncle,"* I never would've thought in a million years something like that could happen to me. It never would've popped into my head. So when I think about kids that are put in that situation, it's like a bad feeling because you trust and look up to these adults. A kid is thinking in that moment, *"Oh this must be okay,"* but in actuality it's wrong. I just don't see how adults do that or what could be going on in the kid's mind, looking up to that adult.

Then I heard my cousin tried to "get" his brother, which I think is more of a male strength thing. I don't think that really had anything to do with sexuality. You never know. A couple of years ago, they got into a fight. I think his brother cut him on the neck with a razor. I asked the question, *"Why do they have so much animosity between each other? Where did all of this come from?"* That's when my mother explained to me that she thinks it started a long time ago when he tried to "get" his brother. But it was never taken any further than that. So I don't know if it was brought up in the family. I know a lot of things that go on in each house and certain aunts talk. I don't think its anything anyone else knows about.

Mrs. Walker makes an important statement by revealing that adults in her family freely engaged in incestuous behavior. In instances such as this, the incestuous behavior is not abusive between two consenting adults. Mrs. Walker delves deeper by admitting that if her father had asked her to do something as a child, she would have done whatever he asked because of her trust in him. We need to understand this is how most incestuous abuse occurs. Adults have the trust and access to children within close proximity, so it is easy to get them to do what is asked, even if it is something as horrific as child sexual abuse.

Jim Hopper is a renowned clinical psychologist, researcher and instructor in psychology at McLean Hospital and Harvard Medical School. His review of research studies ending in 1996 approximated that one in six boys will be sexually abused by the age of 16.[18] Imagine what the rates are now? During Paul's interview, his body language changed, as well as his tone of voice, when I asked him about child sexual abuse in his family. He no longer made eye contact, his voice tone dropped, and he appeared stiff. At the very least, the topic made him visibly uncomfortable.

Patricia's statement that the fight between her cousin and his brother has nothing to do with sexuality is inaccurate. Increased sexual aggression on the part of males can result from being a victim of sexual abuse.[19] People often mistake the sexual aggressive behavior as normal male development. However, the reasoning Patricia may have used to arrive at her conclusion is understandable.

In addition to being a violent sex crime, rape is also about power, domination and control. A man who has anal sex with other men is viewed by many people as not being a "real" man. In prison culture, a man is labeled as another man's "bitch" if he is penetrated anally and the sexual act is not reciprocated. If Patricia's story about her cousins is true, one brother could have been trying to emasculate and control the other by anally raping him. Yet, he could have also proved his "manhood" with a simple fist fight. His attempt to degrade his brother sexually is a reflection of deep-seated sexual issues and something he himself may have experienced at some point in his own life. Children and teenagers who sexually abuse a peer or someone younger than them usually do so because it is a behavior they learned directly from someone else.

RYAN FAMILY

Mrs. Ryan

A lot of times abuse does start from the family. I guess because I have heard so much about it, now it doesn't surprise me. A while back, I guess I would have a question mark behind that. It's very wide open today. A lot of the material and discussion that you read says it does start with family and friends. Some of it could be your own friends.

I would say that there have been some incidents back when the kids were young. I guess you could say touching or some little nasty games went on, which to them probably wasn't nothing. There could've been little signs back then. But back then, you didn't know so much about it. Today is more advanced. I'm not saying this is going on now. It was just some little childhood dirt. Sometimes they passed little nasty games on down. No one else in the family knew when it was going on. At first, I was upset when I talked to him [the abuser]. Then you calm yourself down and go face it. He [the abuser] listened.

Mr. Ryan

The larger the family, increases the chance of incest. The incident in my family was something that happened while babysitting my kids. It was a relative, an uncle. As a father, it makes you feel like you want to do something. Sometimes it bothers me but you have to go on. I let him [the abuser] know I didn't like it.

Otis

I heard statistics on incest less than three months ago. I wasn't surprised. I remember my mom making sure I wasn't running off around the store when I was young but there was never a sit down talk about what to do if someone did this or that. I haven't heard of anything in my family.

Mr. Ryan was more open than his wife in disclosing what happened within his immediate family. Mrs. Ryan's vagueness is common and symbolizes a dilemma many families face when they must accept the reality that their child was harmed by someone in the family.

Otis is aware of the prevalence of incest. As a child, his mother made sure he was in a place she could see him when they were in stores. This is a safety precaution parents take so their child is not kidnapped by a stranger. What precautions are families taking to make sure their children are not vulnerable to incestuous abuse at home?

DAVID PETERSON

<u>Mr. Peterson</u>
Yeah, it does surprise me. Shit! To me, there's only one way I live my life. I consider me living my life righteous. When you talk about incest and foolin' around with one of my kids—no! That's sickening! I haven't heard anything like that happening in my family.

Mr. Peterson is fortunate if nothing like this has happened in his immediate family. However, incestuous abuse has occurred within his extended family. Similar to Paul, his body language also changed when asked this question. It is very seldom that men will disclose inappropriate sexual acts they experienced while they were young, let alone any sexual abusive behavior they experienced at the hands other men.

Chapter 7

Where Do We Go From Here?

I believe it is fair to say that most people in this country are appalled and even disgusted by the sexual abuse of children. Everyone has an opinion of how the problem should be handled. On January 18, 2007, another special episode of the *Oprah Winfrey Show* aired, featuring the families of two abducted boys who were rescued by the police. Dr. Clint Van Zandt, a former FBI profiler, made this comment regarding the laws: "*This is a perfect example of the need for a one-strike law. Anyone who offends against a child, a woman, a man—kidnapping, sexual assault—they go away and they never see the light of day again! One strike, you're gone.*" He was very passionate when he spoke and the audience erupted in applause, showing their agreement. Oprah agreed with Dr. Van Zandt, saying, "*That's what we want. That's what I want to work towards.*" She asked her television viewers to join her in changing the laws. Once laws are changed, will there be an increase in the number of people pressing charges against their relatives?

What do you do if you discover that someone you love in your family has violated your child? The complexity of finding an answer and solution to this question is shown in the following two questions asked of the Peterson family. Often, people find it easier to give their advice about what to do when child sexual abuse happens in someone else's family than when they are dealing with it themselves. With relative ease, members of the Peterson family came up with various suggestions on how to handle child predators and the children who are victimized, until it became personal.

What do you think should be done for/to the perpetrators of child sexual abuse and the children they victimize?

How would you respond if one of your children told you about being sexually abused or was abused by someone in the family?

COLE FAMILY

Mrs. Cole
    I definitely think the child should go through counseling. Maybe participate in a group where you could talk about the situation like AA [Alcoholics Anonymous]. AA talks about your drinking situation. There should be a group where kids can discuss those things and let them know, *"You are not the only person this has happened to."* A group situation through a hospital or church could be set up. Definitely, have a physical with the proper health authorities. Try and make them feel better about the sexual abuse. 'Cause I think a lot of times, when that

happens, kids are blaming themselves. They may think they are the cause of it or led someone on.

I think perpetrators need help also. They need a group set-up situation. If it's something that they've done over and over though, maybe they should just hang 'em if they are a repeat offender [laughing]. If you've gone through these groups and you had counseling and you still don't get it, then you should be hung. I think they should go to jail, stay there and throw away the key [laughing]. Seriously, if you keep doing something over and over, you need to do something to make them understand. I don't really believe in killing anybody. I think that is something God should handle with that person, no matter what you've done. If you kill another person, God should still be the person to judge. Perhaps while they are in jail, insist that they do counseling.

If my girls came to me as kids to say they were abused by family, first, I would let them know I believe them. Two, I'd think, *"No, no. Are you sure? Are you kidding?"* You almost wouldn't take it seriously. That's another way for it to keep continuing because you didn't take the child seriously. The child is out there fending for his or herself... I would have actually sat down with them. I don't know if I would've been able to confront the person that started the situation. I may have to go get some help and find out how you handle somebody like that. Do I just go and confront them or do I talk to my church first to get some ideas on how you handle this? I really don't know how you would handle the person that is doing wrong. But knowing me, I probably would have run on out there and just confronted him. And, of course, you know it's going to be that person's word against my child's word.

You really need to trust and believe the child. I think when it happens, a lot of times parents don't believe it. The child is not going to come to you again, so it just continues on. If it was my husband, I would confront him. I would still listen to the child. I would have to gather some courage and maybe I'd even say, *"Are you sure?"* and see if it would happen again. And after a second time, I would have to confront the person. I'd have to ask them, *"I'm hearing this. Is this true? What's going on? Can you explain it to me?"* and at least give that person an option by doing that. They probably would deny it and say it's not true.

If my daughters told me something now, I'd get my gun [laughing]. Oh mercy! I think it would be the end of my marriage. I don't know. I really feel I would confront the person. If it wasn't my husband, I'd have to think about it. I might just forget about it, if it was long ago—and they don't have a relationship with them. But if that person was bothering somebody else's kid, I might pull the parents aside and tell them to be careful and watch out because in the past this has happened. I don't have any proof of it, but this has happened in the past.

I'd almost have to be in the situation. I might be mad enough to confront the person with my gun for real. It just depends on who it is. If they are dead, then of course, you know there is nothing you can do. Does this person already have a family? If they have a family, then it might be something the other parent may want to watch out for within their own household.

Mr. Cole

Well, for kids up to 12, support and information is needed. Informational support for kids that young could be very limited. When you go over 12, it's just all information. A different type of support, as far as preventing unwanted pregnancies for kids over 12, may be needed. And then, abuse could be within the same sex. Me and my brother-in-law were talking about that. He told me about a case with one guy and a three year-old. Just to imagine something like that... It was just so sad to see somebody actually have a relationship with babies. Of course, there's a difference between a three year-old and a 17 year-old. There are different ways to support and talk about the things that happened.

Of course, lock up the predators. Give them certain support if the crime warrants it. For rape, take them to jail. For abusing small kids, five to twelve, they automatically go to jail. Certainly, predators need some help. You find some of the predators say, *"No matter if you wanna lock me up or whatever, I was born this way. I can't change. I'm going to keep doing it time and time again."* But I think certain states are passing laws now where, if this person has been arrested three times and in jail three times, that's the limit. You can lock them away for the rest of their lives. It's just that society can't let them out there because they will do it again and again. Some of them will admit it. So they need medical and psychiatric support. Maybe new medicines are out. Society just lets 'em out now around these little kids, and they can't control it. There must be something out there to help them with. If you can't, then lock 'em away.

If my daughter came to me saying she was abused, first, I would try to see if I could help it stop. I guess the child would have to be of a certain age to come and ask that. Hopefully, if you see it, you stop it and try to get support for this person who was doing it. If it was the spouse, you'd have to get help. It's not try; it would have to be done. Depending on what it was, you go beyond just you and your spouse. On my wife's side, if her parents were living, I'd see if they were capable of helping her. It'd be kinda tough to keep the son or daughter away from the spouse. I'd have to think about that. Do you split up the family to stop it? I guess, in some respects, it might come to that if the spouse is sick in a way that you can't stop them. If that person kept coming around and didn't want to stop, you could have the law come in—if it's extended family. If it's immediate, then you have to look at it differently. You get support and split up ASAP [as soon as possible] if you can't stop it from happening. You have to deal with it.

If this was something in the past, first, I would ask if they are asking me for help now to go back and get this person who did it. Did this person approach them again? I'd find out exactly what the situation was now. Then I would step in and make sure it didn't happen again on my part or get the law in there to make sure that doesn't happen again. If it's something that has stopped, I'd ask, *"Do you want me to pursue this person? Why are you coming to tell me now? You just want me to know but don't want me to go further with it? How do you want me to help you now? Or is it just for information?"* If this person approached her again saying, *"Do you remember what we did when you were eight years old?"* and tried to renew it or anything like that, I'd do something. After 10 years, some predators try to renew the relationship. I know it happened with certain live-ins and steps. They think, *"Since it's not mine, I can do certain things."*

There wasn't anything that happened in our family structure. I know of stuff with nieces and nephews.

With the way society is set up now, there is probably something that happened within our family that I don't know anything about. I'm sure if I was doing interviews and I digged enough, something would come up.

Emily

In my studies, I've been led to believe people only abuse because they were. I guess I probably have more compassion for an abuser than other people would. I feel like the only way abusing is a consistent thing in a predator's life is if it happened to them. I don't like the fact that it goes on, or that they would do the same thing to someone else that made them feel very uncomfortable or wasn't good in their life... Knowledge is still key in this case. Much therapy and discussion would be necessary for the predator and victim. The victims should have whatever they feel they need to get past it. They mostly need counseling and to be made to feel okay. I know from studies, there's a web of other things caught up in the abuse, including them not wanting to tell.

Everybody needs much prayer and much assistance in that case. I don't think going to jail is the key. I think they have to always account for themselves from that point on—somehow some way. I really don't think the perpetrators can help themselves. I'd give the victims any kind of counsel, medicine—whatever it would take.

If family did this to my child, my first inclination and feeling would be to harm whoever did it. You want to know and you know you can't find out what happened by coming up to the person with your hand around their neck. I'd want it exposed, but it would really depend on who the family member was and how big and bad it got. The right thing to do would be to expose it. But everybody's going to feel ashamed about it. I'd be ashamed to bring it forward to whoever it was, especially if it's one of my elders I respected. Even in the situation I mentioned earlier, I don't know how to bring that up again. I don't know how I would bring that up to anybody.

I'd give my child whatever they needed. They would not be around that individual. I'd probably be very artistic in my way of not allowing it. I'd be angry. I'd be mad. Honestly, my family wouldn't see me. We'd stay around my friends and white people who I know I could trust [laughing]. I know it's not safe, even when you cross color lines. It's just not safe for kids.

Heather

Perpetrators should be locked up and get some counseling. They should never be allowed to be around the child no matter what their relationship is. Kids should be pulled from the home and get counseling. I'd prefer they go to another family member's home instead of a foster home. I guess that's hard, depending on how bad the abuse was. The kid should never see the abuser again. As far as the kids are concerned, that person is dead. It's important for kids to deal with the issues as much as they can so it doesn't hold them back. Sometimes people kick it under the carpet, which doesn't do any good.

If someone in the family did that to my child, I'd kill them. I couldn't really kill them, but some type of harm would happen. My first thought is to protect my child. I could confront them, but it wouldn't make a difference because they'd probably lie. Nothing the abuser could say or do would make me not want to kill them. The abuser would probably try to say,

"Well you don't know what he or she did to me," and I don't want to hear that.

<u>Katherine</u>

For some, if the perpetrator is a man, I think their dicks should be cut off. Some people say child molesters have a disease. I don't know if rehab would help them. Some people say counseling—but I don't think that helps everyone. A support group would be helpful for people who've been abused. Can you give a person like *that* therapy? If the person is an introvert, they wouldn't want to share what happened to them. Extroverts would deal with it better.

If I had kids, I'd want to confront whoever did something like that, but I guess I'd be confused. Gosh, what an argument! I avoid confrontation at all cost. Man, I'd be mad! Shit, do you throw them in jail? After all, they are family. I don't know. Something has to be done. I guess I'd talk to my mom. My poor child...

When the Cole family was asked how perpetrators and victimized children should be handled, everyone had clear solutions. Mrs. Cole believes a support group setting for abused children and the perpetrators would help. Mr. Cole believes all perpetrators should go to jail and the age of the abused child should be considered in the punishment. Emily differs in her opinion, believing jail is not the answer. Heather thinks jail and counseling is necessary for perpetrators while Katherine expresses much more anger, suggesting castration for a male perpetrator.

When it comes to the question of their own children being abused by a family member, the rules of engagement change. Heather expresses her feelings of wanting to confront and kill the person but jail is not mentioned. Katherine admits not knowing what to do because they are family. Emily also expresses ambivalence, saying she would stay away from the perpetrator and give her child whatever (s)he needs.

Mr. and Mrs. Cole give very extensive answers to these questions. They probably have more to say than their children because their daughters do not have children of their own. Mr. Cole is the only person who mentions bringing in the authorities as long as it is someone in the extended family. He would not prosecute anyone in his immediate family. Many parents in this position would respond the same way.

Mrs. Cole appeared to be taken aback at the thought of her daughters being abused by someone in the family. She verbalizes the shock and disbelief she would feel. In one statement, she says she almost would not take her child seriously. Later on, Mrs. Cole says you need to trust and believe the child. She answered the first question in this chapter, stating that perpetrators of child sexual abuse should go to jail. Like her daughter, Heather, she does not mention jail as a solution for the occurrence of incestuous abuse in her own family. The Cole family is an excellent example of the many mixed emotions a person could feel when sexual abuse within a family is exposed.

WALKER FAMILY

<u>Mrs. Walker</u>

Well, an abused child would need verbal counseling. Someone would really need to work with that child. Even though it is a child, the counselor would have to get into the child's mind to see exactly how long it has affected them. Hopefully, it would be someone who has patience and can strengthen the child mentally so he or she is able to move on.

To be honest with you, the perpetrator would need more counseling than the child that was actually molested. Because it's obvious they are missing something. If not, they would not have done what they did. That person definitely needs counseling—there's no ifs, ands or buts about it. I'm not sure of what type, but that person definitely needs to know the things they are doing are really harmful and could hinder a child the rest of his/her life. The counselor would really have to get deep into the person's mind to see and know why they do the things they are doing. Maybe they are doing it because they were brought up where they saw nothing wrong with it. You would have to do a whole lot of digging to find out about this person's background in order to understand where they are right now in their life.

If my kids had come to me when they were young and said someone in the family was molesting them, we would have had to bring that out. Now, if you had asked me this years and years ago, I would not be saying this. What is wrong is when you don't talk about it. The main thing is to learn—be able to teach and help others. But if you are going to make the family member some type of scapegoat or make this person seem like the *"bad guy,"* then you are not helping the situation. Nobody is going to tell or talk about anything when you are portraying or viewing them as a negative person in your eyesight or mind. Thinking, *"They are no good. They shouldn't have done this,"* doesn't help. It has to be about learning.

You have to be very open-minded when you are going to look upon something like this. You can't be sitting up there accusing. You have to be able to talk about it in order to move forward. You could talk to some family members about certain things, and some family members you can't. Their mind is not open or ready for it. Their ears are not ready to hear—even though it is the truth. Some people can condemn and make the situation worse. It would make you wish you had never opened your mouth or feel like you wanna commit suicide. It just depends on exactly who you're gonna talk to if something like this happens within the family. I will give you a good example.

If that happened to me and I had a grandmother, grandfather, my mother and father, those would be the head of the family. I would include them in a "talking circle". That's who I would use if something like that had happened to my son or daughter. I would be able to counsel my son or my daughter myself. But if we had to bring this out in the family, I would want to use the "talking circle". I feel like they, the elders, could be a strong asset to whatever is going on because they've been here longer than we have. They may be able to share that this was something that happened in their past.

If my son or my daughter was telling me now as an adult, my questions to them would be, *"Does it affect you now? Why wasn't it talked about earlier? If you didn't talk about it earlier, what has made you come and tell me now as an adult? Where are we going with this now? Do you feel like it has a hold on you, as far as within yourself? Is it something that you feel like you need to open up about in order to be able to move on?"* I would have to see exactly what their intentions are. That's "touch and go" because I would have to sit down and feel where they are coming from. I would have to find out from my son or my daughter, *"First of all, how many years ago was this?"* Obviously, if they wanna talk about it now as an adult, it's something they still have on their mind.

Sometimes, everybody in your family cannot be trusted. You have to be very careful with certain things because you can do more damage to that victim if you're not careful. You have to think because sometimes you can make matters worse. You have to be very selective about things when it's your life. You may need to talk about it, but you don't need to talk to the world about it. Now, if you are on a talk show and you feel like you wanted to help somebody or you knew of a friend who was in the same situation, it's okay to use yourself. You don't have to use names, but you can say, *"I was a victim within my family."* The person who abused you, hopefully, will be able to come down in the talking circle with you. That person will know who he or she is. Everybody doesn't need to know. If the victim and person who did the abusing were sitting down, talking in the circle, I think a lot of things could be shared.

I'm gonna close with this... I always feel in a family of sons and daughters, brothers and sisters or cousins, you are going to experiment somewhere in your family with sexuality. Just like people say exploratory surgery—I say "exploratory sex," whether your finger is walking on your sister's body or your cousin's body. You're going to learn somewhere. I can remember when we were growing up in the same household, and I noticed my brother whip out his private [penis]. I noticed he was standing with his, holding it. I couldn't put two and two together. We [girls] sat down; we didn't hold ours [vagina]. You notice a difference in the human body right there. You start getting curious as you grow older. How does it function? How does it work? What do you do to make it get an erection? What do you do if you were to penetrate? Your mind doesn't know. The only way you can contribute and get involved in life is if you do something and experience it. Even if it's wrong, you're gonna learn something from it.

I can remember when I was real young, me and my cousin experiencing one another. And right now today she may not be able to talk about it, but I can very easily talk about it. We were two females exploring each other's body. I'd rather it had been my cousin instead of me going out into the street and exploring somebody I didn't know. We were young, maybe nine or eleven. She was the closest thing. I was the closest thing to her. I didn't see anything wrong with what she was doing. And I'm sure she didn't see anything wrong with what I was doing.

To be very honest with you, I didn't know what I was doing but I learned a lot from her. That's the only way I could put it. I learned a lot from her. I think we were really curious to see if we were going to get an erection. It's funny, but it's the truth. If you start poking around in that circle, you wanna know exactly what's going to happen. Didn't nothin' happen.

I guess after I got older, I learned about orgasms and when certain things take place after this and that. But growing up, we didn't know anything. We were kids. We were curious. To be honest with you, I was curious about a boy's body. But I couldn't go to my brother and say, *"Could we do this?"* I would just peep. That was about as far as you could go with it.

Right now, to this day, I still wouldn't say anything was wrong with it. I'm the type of person who wants to know. I learn by my hands being on things—hands on, not off. I got to have "hands on" to know what works and don't work. Everybody is different. It depends on how you look at it. If you were raised when things were secret, sexuality wasn't explained to you properly. You're going to have mixed emotions. You're going to have a whole lot of things working against you. I went through that even after I was married.

Paul

It's kinda hard to say what should be done for molested kids. I guess it would have to depend on the situation they've been through. Some kids have been through certain parts, and some kids haven't been through certain parts. So I could only say the help would have to be based on exactly what they have been through. That's kinda hard.

I don't know about the ones who molested the kids because it would all depend on whether they've done it before. I'm not sitting here saying I condone it. But if I was in the courtroom on the jury, I would base the sentence on if the perpetrator had did it before. Was it just a sick person? What was his intention in doing it? It's kinda hard. I can't sit here and say, "*Aw, well, you know you're a bad person, so you should die or go to jail for the rest of your life,*" because we only got one God. So I can't sit there and play God.

If it happened to one of my kids, I'm gonna wanna know what happened, how it happened, when it happened and who's involved. That's just natural instinct. I'd just talk to my kids. That's the only thing I could really say. I'm not saying I'll go grab a gun and kill somebody or nothin' like that. That's everybody's first instinct, but you gotta sit down and talk first. When certain things happen, you gotta take that little five to ten minutes and calm yourself down and think. 'Cause when you usually jump to your mind's first conclusion, it's always wrong. You always do or say something and end up regretting it later.

Patricia

I think molested children would need a lot of counseling. They just need somebody to talk too. I'm sure they'd have a lot of questions and a lot of things on their minds. Then they need to be taught the proper way.

In school, I knew a very openly gay guy. He wasn't one of the real flamboyant types, but you knew he was gay. He was cool. Back then, he told us the reason he thinks he's gay is because when he was younger and staying in the projects, this guy had him up on the roof. I don't know what the situation was, but the guy ended up raping him. He said he never talked to anybody about it and just assumed that was the proper thing. That is the way it went. He wasn't taught any better and ended up being gay because he was raped by another man.

So I guess if a child is molested, they need to be taught that it's not appropriate behavior. The person who did it is sick. That's not something natural you just go around doing. They need to be taught the basics on what's right because, as a kid, you go off of what grown people tell you and may think, *"Well, okay, they raped me, so that must be the norm."*

I guess the person that did it needs help. But to me, they need to be off the streets. If you help them, how do you know that they are really not sick anymore? You take that chance. They started the little pedophile thing where you have to register. Who's gonna go register and say, *"Hey, I'm a pedophile. Put a big red flag in my front yard so kids don't come over."* It's not working because most pedophiles repeat the same thing. So why put those kids at risk and have them living next door? You think there is this cool dude next door, you let your kids go ever there and play, and he's really sick! I'm not saying put them in jail. But they need to put them away somewhere, like mental institutions. They have enough money. I guess while they are in there, they need to be worked with. If they can show they're not sick—which I don't know how anybody could tell that—then maybe they could get a second chance. That's my suggestion, an institution for pedophiles.

If my kid was abused by family or a boyfriend, I think I would go crazy. I would probably beat up on myself even though you know you shouldn't. You have to trust somebody, and I guess it should start with family. And if you're dating somebody, you hope you've gotten to know them to a point where you can trust them in some way. I would probably beat up on myself because I'd feel like I messed my child up. I hope my child would be strong enough to come out of it. But if he wasn't, I'd probably blame myself thinking something like, *"Damn, I left him with my brother and look what happened."* I don't know how I would get over that. I'd probably be more messed up than the kid. I'm the parent and it's my job to protect my son. You want your kids to have everything in life and be normal as possible. When you have a child, you need help, whether you're married or not. You have to have outside help. You trust family more than you trust the daycare. If it happened at a daycare, I might deal with it a little better.

If it's a boyfriend, it would mess me up in two ways. One, he misused my trust and hurt my child. Two, obviously he had some type of problem all along and shouldn't have been with me in the first place. He obviously had some type of sexual attraction for kids or was just sick in the head. So I think that would be something we would definitely have to be counseled for. It would probably make me a little over-protective. And I would always say things like, *"Now you do understand that wasn't right—right? You don't go around repeating that to anybody. And you don't let this affect you in moving forward in your life."* You can't take some things back but you can apologize and try to work around it. But that's something that could never be right.

The funny thing is that I think about it all the time as a parent. If I have to leave my son with somebody, I think to myself, *"Is he gonna be okay over here?"* When he's at my mom's house, I'm fine. Pretty much anywhere I let him go, I feel like he's okay. I think dating is one of the hardest things for me since I'm not with my son's dad. So when you bring another man in, you hope they have the same interest in your kid as you do. But sometimes men have a power struggle. So I hope that doesn't happen in my house because I already know my son is going to be very headstrong. He wants to do what he wants to, and he wants to run it. When you have another man come in the first thing that comes out of their mouth is, "*You not my daddy!*" So then you hope your man is mentally strong enough to be able to talk to your son and bring him down, instead of physically trying to abuse him. Sometimes if the physical doesn't work, it can turn to sexual.

Members of the Walker family made some very powerful statements and suggestions, as well as some disturbing ones. Paul's response to what he would do if someone in the family sexually abused his daughters was not very definitive. His response is troubling because his children are all girls. He is clear in wanting to know the details but did not address how he would handle a family member who committed this crime against his children. When asked how, in general, perpetrators should be dealt with, one of the questions Paul would consider is, "What was his intention in doing it?" While this question is valuable in evaluating a perpetrator's mental health status, it still does not negate the fact that an abusive act was committed against a child or teenager.

Mrs. Walker is very supportive of abused children and perpetrators getting counseling, as well as supporting her own children if they had been sexually abused in the family. She would bring the abuse out in the open if it happened in her family. Yet she begins to waiver at the thought of other adults wanting to disclose that a relative abused them as a child. Mrs. Walker said, "You don't have to use names, but you can say, '*I was a victim within my family.*' The person who abused you, would, hopefully be able to come down in the talking circle with you. That person will know who he or she is. Everybody doesn't need to know."

It takes a great deal of courage for adult survivors of child sexual abuse to come forward and reveal what someone did to them because of the shame and guilt they may have unfairly carried with them since the abuse began. If a survivor wants to tell the truth and name the abuser, it is perfectly within his/her right and prerogative to do so. What is in the best interest of a survivor's healing varies from person to person. There can be a great deal of empowerment gained after the victim confronts the abuser, regardless if family support is given.

Mrs. Walker was not educated about her body or sexuality as a child. Sexually experimenting with her cousin when they were nine or eleven years old was a healthy experience for her. This happens much more than people realize. All incidents of incestuous behavior are not abusive. Diana Russell did an excellent job exploring this issue by including a chapter in *The Secret Trauma* titled, "Can Incest Be Nonabusive?" She states the following, "When brothers and sisters or cousins who are peers engage in mutually desired sex play, it is not abusive."[20] Therefore, Mrs. Walker was correct when she made the statement that sexual exploration can occur within a family because of children's natural curiosity. However, there is a fine line between innocent exploration or curiosity and sexual abuse. When families have open and honest communication with their children and teenagers about sexuality and personal boundaries, they are in a better position to understand the difference.

Patricia believes there should be an institute for pedophiles. Several people in the Peterson family have mentioned pedophiles. What most people do not understand is that when an adult sexually abuses a child or teenager, that does not make her or him a pedophile. There is a difference between someone with a compulsion (s)he cannot control versus an opportunist who takes advantage of a situation to victimize someone. According to the Diagnostic and Statistical Manual of Mental Disorders (DSM-IV), Pedophilia is when a person has at least six months or more of recurrent intense sexually arousing fantasies, sexual urges or behaviors involving sexual activities with a child or children (usually age 13 or under). Acting on these urges causes the pedophile distress and the pedophile must be at least 16, and five or more years older than a child of 13 or younger.[21] However, not all pedophiles act on their urges and fantasies to abuse children.

There are many perpetrators of sexual abuse. If every guilty person was put in an institution for pedophiles, we would lose many men (and some women) in our own families. We misuse the pedophile label so often it makes one wonder if we would still apply it to a family member. What if you found out a 17 year-old boy in your family was sexually abusing his 13 year-old sister? How about your aunt sexually abusing her 14 year-old nephew? These are tough questions many people are afraid to address until it happens. Even when sexual abuse has happened, it is difficult to accept. Incestuous abuse is similar to sexual abuse outside of the family because of one person's use of power, control, manipulation and sometimes violence to victimize and abuse another individual. This is also prevalent in same sex abuse among males.

Since homosexuality among males was mentioned, it is important for men to pay attention to this paragraph. If another man or boy has been sexually abused or molested, that does not mean he is more prone to living a homosexual lifestyle than any other man. In the case of Patricia's friend, he believes being raped by a man played a significant role in his sexual development and orientation. There is little doubt that it did for him. However, sexual abuse is not the cause of sexual orientation, although it can play a part in one discovering and developing his/her sexual identity.[22] Men and boys who have been sexually abused by other men sometimes make the mistake of internalizing the behavior of the sexual predator, assuming that they must be homosexual if the man chose them in the first place. Most men who have abused boys identify themselves as heterosexual. However, if these same men are diagnosed or classified as pedophiles, their orientation is pedophilia due to their sexual attraction to children.[23]

RYAN FAMILY

Mrs. Ryan

People are trying to get on top of this child abuse and do something about it so it won't be so widespread. Some of the folks have been arrested and stood trial. I think the parents need to get to the bottom of the situation because if you don't, it will continue on and on and on and on. It needs to be stopped. As a child, you don't want that. As a child, you may not fully understand it. Sometimes, as you grow older and it's being talked about more, you feel and understand you didn't like it.

Well, as I said previously, if my kids told me they were abused while they were young, I would try to deal with it—providing I knew about it. I would try to talk to that person and the child. If it seems like it's putting the total weight on the kids, I'd get them some counseling. After all, when you get counseling, it's not something you do out of the ordinary. This is something to help you express your feelings, thoughts or see if this is what "it" was.

Now that my kids are grown, I think I may not have a good feeling if they told me they had been abused way back when, especially if it wasn't brought to my attention, and it's just coming out today. I would try to live through it. If it was a husband, grandparents or anybody, I would want to still love them as family—even if this did occur and we didn't know anything about it. I would still try to find a decent way to deal with it, especially if it was a long time ago. If the one who did it is a loving person deep down on the inside and they care, I think I could deal with it. In fact, sometimes things are better to deal with sooner or later instead of leaving things unsaid. Way back when, it was a little bit harder to deal with, especially if it was something still lingering on.

<u>Mr. Ryan</u>

Most kids know sexual abuse is wrong. If a kid told me they were abused, I would put myself in their situation and tell them how I overcame. My brothers and sisters asked me to do something, but I didn't do it. Show the victims, *"You weren't the only one."* I still talk to my people and don't have a grudge about it. If I do, I keep it to myself.

Grown folks who molest need to be locked up. I don't know if something is wrong with the mind. Once they are behind bars, the same thing will happen to them—an "eye for an eye." Now, if my kids told me somebody in the family did something to them, I would call the authorities. If it was my wife, it'd just be a divorce. If it was female on male, it wouldn't be as bad to me. I'd go and talk to her, but I wouldn't call the police.

<u>Otis</u>

The abused child should be educated on what frame of mind the predator is in. Let the child know they will be okay. Explain to them why people do this because the child will have questions. Let the child have access to resources to get over and out of the situation.

For the predator, it depends on the profile. You can never know if it's their first time or not. You can be a speeder and only have one traffic ticket. If it's one time, they need to be isolated, evaluated and educated to see if they will not repeat the offense. I think after three times you shouldn't ever get out of jail. If a predator kills a child, their life should be taken. It sends a message to other potential predators. After you are a repeat offender and kill someone, I don't think there's no help after that. I don't think we taxpayers should have to pay for him.

If my kids told me family did something to them, I would be enraged, at a loss and confused. I'd gather my mind to understand why this person did this. I'd call and confront the person. Hopefully, it would have been accidental and a first time where authorities wouldn't have to be involved. Counseling is obviously needed. If the person doesn't admit to it and the child was traumatized by it, I'd have to get the authorities. I want to be in control of the consequences. The person may say nothing is wrong with them and refuse to get counseling. Even if it was just a bump, I don't want to play down how serious it was to the child. If my wife was the person, I'd handle it the same way.

Similar to Mrs. Walker, Mrs. Ryan echoes her sister's comments, saying that if a family member abused her child, she would still want to love the perpetrator. Forgiveness is powerful and very freeing. However, these comments are still disturbing because no one says what will happen to the abusive relative. Does the relative get a pass to come around the family in spite of the discomfort it may bring to the abused child? The child's safety, comfort and well-being should be placed above all else.

Mr. Ryan incorrectly assumes children know sexual abuse is wrong simply because he chose not to engage in questionable behavior with his siblings when he was young. Every child is different. Mr. Ryan also reveals his gender bias. He would call the authorities on any male family member who abused his children, but not on his wife or another female relative. Yet, there are, in fact, men who were sexually abused by women in their childhood and traumatized by the experience.

I met a man who was sexually molested by a preteen girl, who was his babysitter, when he was five years old. Now he realizes she was probably being abused by men in her family. Another gentleman was sexually abused by his aunt. He expressed strong emotions as he revealed how uncomfortable it made him feel. As a teenager, he did not know any better. He buried the secret for a long time and did not tell his mother what happened until 20 years later.

Otis' response of hoping the sexual abuse incident was "accidental" so the authorities would not have to be involved is a common reaction of denial. Many parents want to believe the abuse was innocent child's play or a "mistake," perceived in the wrong way by the child. Fortunately, Otis said he would not minimize the effect on his child, whether the incident was *accidental* or not. His example demonstrates what it means to put the child's feelings first. Unlike his father, Otis would not give his wife preferential treatment if she had abused one of their children.

DAVID PETERSON

<u>Mr. Peterson</u>

For one, if a parent were to do that to their child, to me that parent is a sick person—a very sick person. They should receive help. If they don't receive the proper help, lock them up. Because the kids are what I consider the victims. You have to give them everything that you can give them as far as help. A person who commits something like that... One time when I was young... I would have one thing in my mind—kill 'em! You should *never* put your hands on a child.

If a family member inappropriately touched my kids, the first thing I would say is, *"Who did it?"* If I was given the right answer, I would not go and attack the person. I would go to that person and tell them, *"You are a sick ass person. You need prayer."* I would be very shocked if my wife did something like that.

Mr. Peterson exemplifies a common reaction an adult verbalizes at the thought of a parent sexually abusing his/her own child. He seemed like he was about to allude to something more, but then stopped himself and expressed outrage, saying, "Kill 'em!" Yet, once the general question about sexual abuse turns personal, he does not express killing a relative who does this to his child. Instead, he makes it clear that he would *not* attack the person and simply tell the person how sick (s)he is.

What does this do for the child and the family as a whole? We can continue to do little or nothing and remain silent. The result will be an increasing number of children growing into adults who numb themselves with drugs, food, sex or even suicide. A review of research studies conducted by Paul Mullen and Dr. Jillian Fleming, found that a history of child sexual abuse can result in an adult experiencing higher rates of substance abuse, eating disorders, depression, anxiety and post-traumatic stress disorders.[24]

The first step to empower families after sexual abuse has been disclosed is to address the immediate needs of the child. In other words, act on behalf of the child or teenager's physical, emotional and mental health needs first, in order to keep the cycle of abuse from continuing. Unfortunately, this is where many families fall short.

Chapter 8

Does Culture Matter?

In Chapter 7, members of the Peterson family grappled with trying to imagine how they would handle incestuous abuse happening within their own families. At the end of their interviews, it was necessary to elicit responses that went beyond what we covered in our discussions thus far. The last question was asked at the end of the interview with the intention of understanding the Petersons' knowledge about the impact incestuous abuse can have on African American children.

While there has been considerable research on the occurrence, effects and treatment of child sexual abuse, researchers in the Department of Child Development and Family Studies at Purdue University show that most research does not take ethnic and cultural oppression into consideration.[25] Do the Petersons believe there is anything unique about being an African American in the United States that may prohibit them from disclosing incestuous abuse? With no prodding, some individuals did mention oppression and slavery in their answers.

Why do you think African American families don't discuss or disclose child sexual abuse when it happens within their family?

How do you think an African American child who has been victimized within the family is affected when no one acknowledges or deals with what happened?

COLE FAMILY

<u>Mrs. Cole</u>

It all comes back to the fact that families don't want anyone to know. If somebody is on drugs, they don't want anyone to know about it. They purposely keep it quiet. It's the same thing with alcohol abuse. I think people just don't want the stigma. We have to learn to understand that sometimes it's good to share because other people can benefit from it. Or we have to stop that person from doing it. If the abuse is a secret, then that person is probably going to continue to do it.

I think the child's age determines how much they understand. It could make them very resentful, bitter, angry or withdrawn. If you are really young, you may not understand the fact that, *maybe it's not my fault.*

<u>Mr. Cole</u>

The slavery set up was designed to make the Black family structure weak. Blacks needed to be *hush-hush*. The Black female's role in controlling the family at that time was a little different, which was the way slave owners wanted it. So the female was held down because of that. This is why sexual abuse wasn't told. Maybe it wasn't supposed to get out in order to keep from showing weaknesses in the family group. The Black male was seen as weak because he didn't have control over anything.

Society will keep Black people down if they can. General society is more lenient than Blacks are. White people tend to accept things out there. They just put up with it. They do things like that. Some of them won't, but some of them do. If you go over to Africa, I don't think it's acceptable. If you look at Blacks and whites, I think sexual abuse is higher in white communities. Then again, things change and now Blacks accept more, especially the younger generation.

I also think the Willie Lynch Syndrome[*] contributed to us not telling certain things. There was a set of rules or questions set up by old slave owners 300 to 400 years ago. It said if you did certain things to slaves, they'll react in a certain way. There were about 10 different steps that said if you kept doing these things, they'll never change. If you read about the things they said like, *"You don't let them get as much education,"* everybody who is 35 and older can relate and see the results of the Willie Lynch Syndrome still out there. I think every Black child at a certain age can see this and change within themselves. Just to know that this is what was expected of us back in those days makes you try to change and do the best you can.

---

[*] The Willie Lynch Syndrome is a term that sparked national dialogue in the African American community in 1995 after Minister Louis Farrakhan delivered his address at the Million Man March. Minister Farrakhan quoted a speech supposedly written and delivered by white slave owner William Lynch in 1712. Lynch allegedly visited America in order to help Virginia slave owners control their slaves. There is no valid proof that this letter or speech ever existed. Many reputable researchers and historians of African American history and studies have deemed it completely false.

The effect the abuse has on the Black child depends on how you are going to support this child. The child may need psychiatry. You really have to show as much love as you can. Hopefully, the child will grow up normal and try not to be affected by it. Love and support is all you can do. Make sure it doesn't happen by not putting the child in situations where it might happen again.

Emily

I know there has to be shame in general, no matter what family it is. But as for Blacks, I honestly think they don't think that it happens. I have a girlfriend who was abused. An older uncle petted her wrong. She told her parents immediately and the uncle was dealt with. So, I definitely know it exists. I don't think many families do. I don't think whites are any more open about incest than we would be. But I think a lot of ours goes back towards slavery days. I think we always viewed ourselves as families. A lot of the pulling away, being sent away and not being made to feel like we were family could have something to do with it. Back then, we would have felt that we put a family member or people we cared about in jeopardy—even for doing wrong like that.

If violators were in my family, I'd still have compassion for them. It doesn't mean that a family member is like "that." But if you find one incident that happened in the family 20 years ago, can you bring that to light now? I think we're inclined to do nothing. Let's say you find out something about a sibling who has a reputation for being such. No one wants a sibling, cousin or anyone in their family labeled as "The Abuser" or "Lester the Molester." Nobody wants to say that because of the type of offense that it is. I think that's it. It's one thing to hit me. We can openly discuss that. But for *that* type of offense, it's just weird. People are gonna hush up. They're gonna shut up. They're not gonna make it open. Why do we do this? Protection. We're gonna protect our own. Black people have enough problems and issues in society as it is. To not come forward with that kind of stuff doesn't surprise me at all—especially if it's something you have to deal with day in and day out.

If the family knew but didn't acknowledge the abuse, I think the main way it would be expressed by a kid is anger. I would like to believe abuse would not express itself in another generation. If the family knew, who do you blame? The child will express it a lot of ways. They'll be peculiar or withdrawn. They could do weird stuff around other children.

I know you've seen Chris Rock's comedy show when he said, *"Where them kids?! They betta not be in there with Uncle Lester! I told you not to leave them kids in there!"* That was somewhat funny, but it shouldn't have been, because he was telling the truth in all jest. He was telling the truth! I think that all families know that. They know the ones they question. And they know the ones that they tell you to keep an eye on. My mom wasn't one to let her kids stay any and everywhere. I would say it was fair for my mom to be that way. Kids are not safe. I was the type of child who was very quiet and sweet. Honestly, I would've been the perfect candidate for that [sexual abuse]. I wouldn't have probably said anything either unless it was something I couldn't help but say. It would've probably made me sad or would've been expressed other ways like crying, not wanting to stay there—that sort of thing. I think Mom would've seen that... As far as I'm concerned, as careful as she was, I wasn't necessarily safe in the environments I was in. There are still times I could tell you that I thought were questionable. But it was never an abuse—so to speak.

Heather

Maybe families don't say anything because they are embarrassed and think it will go away. But they're just thinking about themselves and not the child. It probably makes the child feel not loved, like no one cares. People try to ignore it instead of confronting it. If the abuser is still around, the abuser will ignore the child and the issue as if it didn't happen. It makes the kid feel not loved, and they'll probably deal with it when they are older. The kid will think they did something wrong when they didn't.

Katherine

I guess Black people are more private. Some might think it's a natural thing, depending on how long it's been going on. Black people might not be educated, but I don't firmly believe that. I think that most people know if someone touches you and it doesn't feel right, something's wrong. My co-worker and I talk about a girl in her first grade classroom who masturbates. When my co-worker asked the girl's mother why her daughter was doing it, the mom's response was, *"She's doing it because we haven't had our 'me' time."* The mother and child are white. Regardless of race, I think incest affects the kid in every area. I see things as a social worker. Grades suffer because they are worrying about stuff. It's just awful. I feel bad for the kids.

Heather and Mrs. Cole did not mention anything specific regarding culture or race when asked why African Americans do not disclose incestuous abuse. Their comments are statements which people of different cultural groups would probably identify. Katherine thinks African Americans differ from other groups by having a tendency to be more private. Emily believes "Black people already have enough problems to deal with." Large numbers of African Americans have gone through negative encounters with the police, criminal justice system and social service agencies. All have a long history of not fully serving and having a negative impact on African American families. Knowing that a perpetrator is in one's family does not decrease the desire to protect the person.

Contrary to what Mr. Cole stated, incestuous abuse is also prevalent in African countries. However, Mr. Cole's connection of slavery to a present day fear of African Americans disclosing incest has validity. During the slavery period, white men controlled African American families. The legacy of white slave owners raping slave women and not being held accountable had a traumatic effect on the families and shaped how they viewed and expressed their sexuality. In Dr. Joy DeGruy Leary's book, *Post Traumatic Slave Syndrome*, she writes,

> *"It was the master who more often than not became the imprint for male parental behavior... and this imprint was passed down through the generations. At its foundation, this imprint was dominated by the*

necessity to control others through violence and aggression... The individuals and families who survived the slave experience reared their children while simultaneously struggling with their own psychological injuries."[26]

African American slave women and men had no choice but to endure while helplessly watching their daughters experience the same sexual violent crimes they had. Now the cycle of sexual violence has been passed down through generations, and African Americans are perpetrating the same crimes against each other that white slave masters committed against their slaves.

WALKER FAMILY

Mrs. Walker
I think something like that happening in the family is very degrading and embarrassing. If it's talked about, I think it stays in the circle where it happened. Certain things are instilled like, "*Whatever you hear in this circle stays in this circle.*" People are afraid they will be looked at in a different way. The person that it actually happened to may be looked upon differently. People may think, "*Could they have prevented it? Could they have avoided it? Why didn't they come forward and say something?*" I think eventually the victim is the one who really walks away feeling like more of a victim than they were previously because of how society looks at things. Society says, "*They knew what they were doing.*" Or people can lie and say, "*She was aware of that. He was aware of that. They came on to me.*" So

you don't want anything like that out in society. I could be wrong, but this is what I think. You're not going to find people talking about it, but I can tell you one incident that happened with one of my close friends.

This incident involved her son, her nephew and her granddaughter. The nephew and son were teenagers. Her granddaughter was a child between the ages of five and six. The nephew and son molested the granddaughter for a long time. Nobody knew about it because they all stayed in the same house. Finally, one day, she told her grandmother not to leave her at home with them because they would do bad things to her and hurt her. Even though her grandmother didn't know what she was talking about, she's the type of person who will find out the whole story, not just bits and pieces. That is just what she did.

She started taking her granddaughter places with her and drilled her for information. Every time the grandmother would leave her granddaughter with the son and nephew, she'd have a fit. The boys had been molesting her for a long time, and told her that she better not talk or tell anyone. So for a long time she wouldn't say anything until they started doing things to her sexually that started hurting her.

The grandmother found out her son and her nephew were molesting her at the same time and doing the same things. Both of them were aware of what they were doing. She happened to call me about it and asked, *"If your child was doing this, what would you do? Would you turn them in?"* I told her, *"If it was my child, I'd have no choice but to turn them in. This is the only way that they will learn. You have to turn something like this in."* Her whole family, the whole family, turned against her because she stood up for what was right. She's deceased now, but her son and nephew did serve time for this. To this day, I still feel like she did the right thing. At the time she would call me, I told her, *"It's a hard role to take on. A lot of times when you are standing for what is right, you will find everybody against you."* She went all the way with it, and I was real proud of her.

I think a child is affected tremendously when it's not discussed. It's almost like a time capsule being kept in a bottle that you can never open. That child would always have this in the back of their mind and have nowhere to unload or tell anybody about it. As long as that child walks around without talking about it, I believe the child will always have a mental effect. The mental effect would go back to the abuse.

When you can talk about it [being sexually abused] openly, not only do you help yourself, but you are helping others. It's healing when you are getting rid of certain things. In the worst scenario you can make some good out of it. You learn by talking, even from the worst thing. Everything doesn't have to be good or positive for you to learn from it. You could also be there to help others by giving advice and use yourself as an example to say, *"I've been through it."* This is when you're really strong. But as long as you're hiding behind certain things, you're not strong. It's like you're a victim within yourself.

Paul

Black people just got a way of ignoring stuff. Or we keep pushing stuff back until either you forget or don't want to talk about it. We'll say, *"Aw, that didn't really happen!"* or brush it off. The kid it happens to can make a choice to do something good or bad. He could dwell on it, which ain't a good thing. Or he could say, *"Hey, that's something that happened to me a long time ago."* Just look at it as a bad point and time in life. Some people take that kind of stuff and make positive things happen. Somebody might go open up a homeless kids' shelter. Or if it was a female who might have been a prostitute, she might become a social worker and work with kids. You could dwell on it and be mad at the world or do something with it. Make something positive out of it.

<u>Patricia</u>

A lot of Black families might not have the resources they need to get the proper help. I think they don't know how to talk about it or they're just not aware of how to communicate certain things and not be ashamed. They try to keep everything on the down low and portray a certain image as if everything is okay, *"We don't want everybody on the outside looking at us as the dysfunctional family on the block."* A lot of times they may not know how to deal with it. So instead of actually confronting the situation, they just try to bury it and move on. Later on down the road, what happened comes out in some other crazy situation. Also, a lot of white people have money to go see psychiatrists and pay a lot to get outside help. I guess the best thing would be to sit down and talk about whatever needs to be said. But, instead, people try to bottle it up and not deal with it. Then the kids end up being screwed up.

If the family deals with the situation, the kid that it happened to may grow from that situation, learn something and grow up to help other people. That's how a lot of people end up helping people because they went through it. They know what steps their family took them through. That's one way the kid can turn out. If the situation isn't dealt with, the kid can have a lot of anger. They can't get through life, can't keep a job, or can't keep friends. They feel like everybody owes them something. They could end up being a hoe [whore], thinking that's the norm or way of life.

You could also end up being confused about your sexuality. Maybe they feel comfortable on both sides—opposite sex and same sex. Some people turn their nose up at that. But if they're comfortable with it, they're comfortable with it. A lot of people say you're born homosexual. I don't believe that personally. I think it's more of a choice. Some people just wake up one day and say that's the choice they want to take. Then other people have had a past sexual experience they've battled with so long, they might not feel comfortable with the opposite sex. So they have to look at the same sex to feel comfortable in a relationship.

In response to answering the question of how an African American child can be affected by incestuous abuse, Mrs. Walker, Paul and Patricia all mention taking a bad experience and turning it into something positive. Of course there is always something to learn from any experience. Today, more and more survivors of sexual assault are speaking out in rebellion to the injustice done against their souls in an effort to heal and take their power back. Some have taken social action by becoming involved politically to make sure state and community resources for survivors are consistently funded and protected. However, an unsupportive abusive upbringing and family environment makes it challenging for individuals to heal enough and turn it around to help others. The numbers of men and women who have become social activists are small in comparison to the numbers of people who still suffer in silence because of the love and support they did not receive from their families.

Patricia believes many families may not have the resources to get help. Some African American families are unaware of what resources are available to them due to limited access and outreach on the part of local and state funded agencies. Rape crisis centers are located in every state and most major cities in America. If outreach is not done in communities of color, those who would be open to utilizing free counseling and support services will continue to suffer alone. White families that can afford private therapists keep incestuous abuse as much of a secret as everyone else. It is still considered taboo to disclose sexual abuse within families in many cultures in the United States.

Patricia is correct when she states that sexual abuse can cause confusion about one's sexuality. However, it does not *cause* a person to be bisexual, as she suggested in her answer. The majority of children and adults who are sexually abused are women and girls. Most of them grow up to live a heterosexual lifestyle. If this were not true, we would have a higher number of bisexual and lesbian identified women. The Rape, Abuse and Incest National Network (RAINN), states, one out of six women have been raped or experienced an attempted rape in their lifetime.[27] Other studies put the number as high as one in four women. It is not uncommon for people to focus on sexual orientation because our community is quick to link certain sexually deviant behaviors with same sex behavior.

RYAN FAMILY

Mrs. Ryan

You know, I think we really want to say something when these kinds of things happen, but there are just so many other things that we got to deal with being Black. White folks are talked about too, but it just seems like Blacks are talked about so badly. This is something that stays in us as we grow up. Sometimes we just say, *"No, let's not go further with anything."* We want to drop it right there. Sometimes other races may not feel that way. They just put it out in the open. It seems like when something went down in the Black race, it was always looked at to be so much lower. Sometimes, they look at us like that anyway. So I would assume when we don't say anything, it's somewhat because of that. But other races are doing it too and probably even more than us—you never know. As far as our folks, I could see why people hold back a little bit.

When families won't help the kids, I think it does affect them in more ways than one. Sometimes, it can come back on you as you grow up—especially if a person doesn't remember it. If you don't get counseling, it could be rough. Some kids are different than the others. Some aren't bothered by it [being sexually abused] whatsoever and just live on through it. Others are really lost.

Mr. Ryan

Maybe the kids this happens to don't say anything because they don't want to hurt their parents. I don't know why we [parents] don't go to the person [abuser] directly. Some kids who went through this grow up and leave the situation alone. But other people use the incident to tease the victimized person. To get over something, you have to forget it. As a kid, you should be able to tell them [sexual predators] it shouldn't happen. A 12 year-old knows right from wrong. He should get away, run, tell or something. Even a five or six year-old knows right from wrong. Even a three or four year-old will run and tell.

Otis

We have so many bad habits, like simply not speaking to someone when you get up in the morning. Not caring for each other enough or showing concern is a bad habit. Not having enough education on how to respond or prevent sexual abuse from happening is a problem too.

Slavery has a little percentage in this problem too; more so the slave master and what he got away with. If my grandmother was traumatized by a white man, someone in her own race or family members, she's not going to want to get into this when she brings up her own kids. Back when I was young, I wanted to talk to my grandmother and mom about certain things, but I felt like I couldn't. Maybe I can now, but it may bring up something and put them in a bad mood.

A kid who goes through this has the mindset of the age you went through it. Not being acknowledged would make things a whole lot worse when there is no outlet or resources. You are out there confused.

Mrs. Ryan and Otis express views similar to Mr. Cole and Emily in regards to slavery and the burden of everyday pressures African Americans face. We can not let apathy be an excuse to do nothing when we know a child or teenager has been sexually violated by a relative. Education on the prevalence of sexual abuse in our communities is important, but it is not enough. When we know sexual abuse has occurred and then refuse to help the children in our families, from that point forward, we become responsible for their ongoing pain and suffering.

Mr. Ryan thinks children may not tell their parents because they are afraid of hurting them. This could be true in some cases. Children do not necessarily come to their parents because statements like those made by Mr. Ryan place the blame and responsibility of sexual abuse on the abused child. He said that a five or six year-old knows right from wrong and a three or four year-old will run and tell. What language does a three or four year-old have to tell an adult that someone in the family is sexually abusing him or her? Children show signs in many ways. We simply are not aware or we ignore them. Bed wetting, crying, withdrawal, school problems, depression, sleeping and eating disorders are only some of the common reactions of sexually abused children and teenagers.

Mr. Ryan also believes children should be able to stop abusers by telling them "it shouldn't happen." How does any 12 year-old or teenager facilitate a conversation with an abusive relative when (s)he has been subjugated to a position of powerlessness and victimization? Whether the child tells an adult or not, (s)he is not responsible for being sexually abused.

DAVID PETERSON

Mr. Peterson

Most Black people were used to dealing with Mr. Charlie. Mr. Charlie was the white slave driver. The white man was the only one who ever got *everything*. He would sit back and rape all the damn people. All this stuff came from him and came down to the Black man having to deal with this. So I believe a lot of Black people just don't believe in discussing things like that. When you can't do nothin' about nothin' you have to have an escape. You know what it is? Just leave it alone. Leave it alone and keep it in your mind. But I think it should be discussed. I made sure my family was not gonna be raised the way I was. My family got love.

Mr. Peterson also echoes the opinions of other people in the Peterson family, naming slavery as one reason African Americans have difficulty disclosing sexual abuse in families. Slaves could not do anything about being sexually abused. They were considered property, and raping Black women was not considered a crime. However, we are now in the 21st century. We can end sexual violence in our community and families. Trying to escape or forget about painful memories and experiences only leads to unhealthy ways of coping. Self-mutilation through cutting one's body, risky sexual behavior and drug and alcohol abuse are a few ways survivors who were not supported try to "escape."

If African Americans believe the origin of our sexuality issues is rooted in our oppression, the fact that we can name it and are aware of it means we are capable of rising above it. With their collective knowledge, there are still secrets within the Peterson family. In many instances throughout the interviews, it was obvious when things were not being revealed or fully shared. The silence and repression attached to sexuality still has power over us. It is time to advance our education and activism to remove the stigma and shame of sexual abuse in order to heal from it. This movement must be expanded to thoroughly examine sexuality in American culture and in the African American community. The mental, emotional, spiritual well-being and survival of our families and future children depend on it.

Chapter 9

My Story

Shortly after I began interviewing a few members of the Peterson family, I decided to answer these questions myself. In 2005, I had someone I trust ask me the same questions, following the same order I used with the Petersons. It was the best way for me to connect with this subject on a more personal level. I have included my answers at the end of the book to give the reader more insight into my own life and experiences. Sometimes, it is easier to analyze other people than to look at one's self. Answering these questions was more awkward than I anticipated. I even considered not including this chapter, but as I recognized the importance of what I am asking the reader to do, I realized how important it is that I lead by example and take the first step.

Where did you receive your first messages about sexuality?

I remember my first messages were from playing with boys at school and TV. I remember watching HBO when I was eight. My parents made a big deal out of not watching rated 'R' movies. When they weren't around, I would watch the HBO channel, particularly a movie called *Porky's*. I felt like I was exposed to an underground world when I saw teenage boys in this movie spying on girls taking showers.

In school, boys would try to kiss me. Actually, Matt was my first kissing partner in preschool. On the days our class got the chance to swim, Matt and I would swim under water and kiss. Then, in first grade, I had a boyfriend named Randall. We would sneak behind the classroom chalkboard and kiss. As far as my parents were concerned, I really don't remember them saying much to me. And, of course, I kept my stolen smooches with my preschool and first grade boyfriend a secret.

What messages did you receive from your family about sexuality?

How have the messages you received from your family affected the way you express your sexuality in the past and present?

When I was eight years old, one of my older cousins, five years my senior, introduced sexual "games" to me. We would have pillow fights and whoever knocked the other person down could do whatever they wanted to the fallen person. When Brad faked being knocked down, I usually tickled him and smashed in his nose. However, when

I was knocked down in the pillow fight, he asked if he could remove some of my clothes. I remember thinking this was weird. In my eight year-old mind, I rationalized that if I had to take off a piece of clothing, then he would too. So after our first round of pillow fighting, I made him take off clothes as well. Before I knew it, we were both jumping up and down on the bed naked. Brad wasn't the only cousin who would watch me. Sometimes Clay would baby-sit too. Clay liked to play house and wanted to practice kissing. My sexual exploration with them continued throughout the summer.

Looking back, I realize I was lucky. There were some unique things about my experience that I didn't find common with people who had been sexually abused or molested. My cousins at the time were certainly manipulative, but I was fortunate that nothing was forced on me against my will. I actually looked forward to being in their company. No penetration of any kind happened. All we did was smooch—lips only, hug and rub. Whenever I didn't want to *play*, we played UNO, checkers or video games. I didn't feel any shame about the experience until I told my mother.

One day, my mother asked me what I did with Brad or Clay. I told her about whatever sexual game we had played that particular evening. She lowered her newspaper, looked over her granny glasses and began to ask me more questions very calmly. I just answered them matter-of-factly. Unbeknownst to me, she immediately spoke with two of my aunts the next day. What was said, to this day, I don't know only because when I inquired recently, she couldn't recall what they discussed. But what I remember clearly of the situation was her coming back and saying to me in a disapproving tone, *"The reason you didn't tell me was because you liked what you were doing."*

I internalized the tone of her voice and felt ashamed. She never brought it up again and my cousins were mad at me for telling. They were still allowed to baby-sit me, but the sexual games and exploration ended. I was lucky. But, knowing what I do now, if I was in my mom's position today, I would not let my nephews continue to watch my children because you never know.

My father let his opinion be known about sex when my sister and I were teenagers. One night, after watching a family movie together, he made it clear to both of us, *"I don't want no babies in this house! You two better be real careful. If you go out there messing around with those knuckle head boys and get yourself in trouble, I'm gonna put you in one of those homes for pregnant teenage girls. I have raised my kids, and I am not taking care of anymore!"* My father made it clear to us that the Bible said we were supposed to wait until we were married to have sex. His upbringing was firmly rooted in Christianity.

The messages I received from my family were helpful because I decided to wait until I was in college to become sexually active. By then, I felt comfortable with myself and my sexuality. I believe my mom's initial extremely calm reaction to me at eight made me comfortable enough to tell her when I was ready to have sex the day before I actually did it. Her attitude made all the difference in the world for me.

My father's beliefs and mine are not the same when it comes to religion and sexuality. I believe the way Christianity is taught represses sexuality and is oppressive to women, depending on who is teaching and interpreting the Bible. We agree to disagree.

How do you think society influences sexuality?

How have the messages that you have received from society affected the way you express your sexuality, past and present?

Society sends conflicting messages about sexuality. On one hand, women are told how they should express their sexuality. If a woman moves outside of the rules that society has set up for her, particularly within her ethnic group, family or spiritual/religious background, she can easily be labeled as promiscuous. There seems to be no grey area for women even today. We are either angels or sluts. The general images depicted in advertising, television, music videos and movies seem to promote hyper-sexuality for both genders. The huge difference is that men are given a symbolic "thumbs up" for being sexually assertive and aggressive. As a Black woman, I don't appreciate it. What does this message say to young kids when it's okay for one gender to be sexually active and the other has to resist and be passive? Meanwhile, men are socialized to be aggressive and sleep with as many women as possible.

In spite of the push for adults to be free and act in any way we choose sexually, society doesn't create a non-judgmental forum for expressing sexuality for kids or adults. Religion had the biggest impact on me when I was growing up. With my father's reinforcement, I held onto to the belief that in order to be considered a good Christian girl and woman, I would remain a virgin until I was married. I saw how girls who were sexually active and pregnant were treated in high school, and I did not want to be one of *those* girls. Because if I became one of them, I would go to hell after I died, and I certainly didn't want that.

How would you teach your children about sexuality?

Would there be a difference between what you would teach your son versus your daughter if you had children of both sexes?

I don't have children. If I did, I would share my view on sexuality and educate them, using language and images they could understand. They would know that having sexual feelings is natural and nothing to be ashamed of. I would also educate them immediately about any negative language or unhealthy behavior I saw them doing. Double standards based on gender would not be tolerated under my roof. Meaning, my son would not be allowed to be out on a date with his girlfriend until midnight while my daughter is expected to be home by 10 p.m. My children would be taught that there is nothing wrong or sinful about wanting to express sexual feelings, as long as two people of a mature consenting age both want the sexual experience and are safe.

While I would not want to put fear into any child, my kids would have to be made aware that some adults and kids get into unhealthy sexual behaviors. We would talk about adults they know, as well as strangers who may try to get them to do sexual things. My children would be taught to use their voice, even if it means disagreeing with an adult. They would know that other people don't have a right to invade their personal space. These conversations would begin happening by age three, as soon as the child can begin understanding how powerful they are.

I remember asking my mom at a young age how women get pregnant. She didn't give me a make believe story about a stork dropping a baby down the chimney. My kids would be told the truth. They would be made to feel as comfortable coming to me as I was with my mother. Pregnancy seems to be a fear for a lot of parents. My message would be the same to any child I had, regardless of gender. It would differ only in the area of sexism. I'd let my son know that the measure of being a man is not in direct proportion to the number of women he sleeps with.

My kids would know the importance of intimacy. They would know the importance of respecting whoever they have an intimate relationship with, sexual or not. They'd also be taught that sexuality is spiritual. The way women are portrayed in the media, expressing themselves just to get a man's attention, is something my daughter wouldn't fall prey to—to the best of my ability.

Did your parents or any adults talk to you about what you should do if someone touched you inappropriately as a child?

Do you know of any past or current incidents of child sexual abuse in general?

My mother could have said something very brief, but it doesn't stand out now, so the message was not strong. What I vividly remember is my mom accusing me of acting strange when I was 13 years old. She asked me if everything was okay. I got the usual teenage questions, *"Are you on something? Are you using something?"* I remember her asking, *"Is your father touching you?"* I guess she was grasping at straws because she asked me on two occasions. I was so horrified and shocked that she would think something like that! After I repeatedly said no and expressed how disgusting it was, she let me know, *"If he or anybody touches you, tell me just like you did with your cousins."* I said okay. Because of that, I always knew if that happened to me, I could tell my mom and she would believe me.

Thank goodness my father was not that kind of man. I never discovered dads would do that to their own kids until I was in my early 20s. I remember questioning why my mother even married my father if she asked a question like that. At that time, I was gravitating more towards my father. We went to church and Bible study. Whether or not my mom was grasping to understand my distance from her at that age, I now realize how much she truly cared about me to ask that question. There are thousands of mothers who suspect the father or father figure of their children is sexually molesting or abusing the kids and say absolutely nothing—even when the child brings it to light.

Sexual abuse is in the media every week. Of all the publicized cases, I was most disturbed by R. Kelly [Rhythm and Blues singer, songwriter and producer]. I believe he is a pedophile and find it sad and disturbing that he continues to get so much community support. One of my favorite radio stations in New York played his song, *Happy People*. At the end of the record the dee jay made the comment, *"Yes, R. Kelly, we'll keep supporting you as long as you stay away from those young girls."* And then the dee jay laughed. He was an older gentleman. I didn't find it funny. When the video tape of R. Kelly having sex with a 14 year-old girl came out in 2002, I remember women I spoke with excusing his behavior, making comments like, *"But he's so talented. He may be a pedophile, but you can't take anything away from his music!"* He hurt girls and he needs help. I refuse to buy his CD or support anyone, famous or not, who takes advantage of children and teenagers by sexually molesting and abusing them. I believe when Black people can honestly look at someone like R. Kelly and plainly say, *"If he did the crime, he must serve the time,"* we will have made significant progress. Until that day comes, people of all ethnic groups and cultures will continue to blame those who are abused and taken advantage of without putting any responsibility on the perpetrator of the crime.

Did you know that incest is one of the most common forms of child sexual abuse?

Have you heard of child sexual abuse happening within your family?

I didn't always know that so much sexual abuse occurs from somebody you know or with a stepdad, uncle, friend of the family, etc. As a child, I was taught to fear the stranger. Now that I'm an adult, I know this outdated assumption makes kids and adults vulnerable. Nine times out of ten, the person that is going to rape or abuse you is someone you know.

PUSH is a book by Sapphire that opened my eyes and made me aware of the problem. I knew adults were raped and children were sexually abused. But until I read this book, I could not imagine adults, siblings or relatives violating each other within their families. Some research studies are now showing that one in four women and one in five boys are sexually assaulted.

Most people aren't reporting incestuous abuse for a variety of reasons. I've listened to story after story of women who do nothing to protect their daughters from the abuser because the man is the primary financial backbone for the household. Most perpetrators are men. People are reluctant to prosecute their own family members. And at the end of the day, due to the racism experienced in the criminal justice system, who would honestly feel at peace sending another Black man to jail? It's easy for someone to say, *"If someone puts their hands on my child, I'm calling the police! I don't care who it is!"* But as a friend of too many survivors of sexual molestation and abuse, I've witnessed their cries fall on deaf ears when they gathered the courage to expose the family secret.

I know of incidents of molestation and abuse within my own family. I'm not at liberty to disclose them without permission from the people involved. I can say, one incident was in the family and another was date rape. I also have a cousin who is serving jail time for raping a preteen who may be his biological daughter. It made me sad to hear that. When I asked my parents how the girl was, neither one knew. I did not grow up around this cousin, but I saw him on a few family vacation trips as a kid. I question the safety of kids and teens in my own family if the adults do not begin to tell the truth about the past to prevent sexual molestation and incest from happening in the future.

What do you think should be done for/to the perpetrators of child sexual abuse and the children they victimize?

How would you respond if one of your children told you about being sexually abused or was abused by someone in the family?

Perpetrators of sexual abuse should be prosecuted. It is a crime. At the same time, they also need psychological help. Many people think individuals who commit these crimes can not be "cured." If men and women who sexually abuse are "sick," it is a reflection of where we are as a society. We will not get better as a people until we address our issues with sexuality. A pedophile is one kind of abuser. Not every man who has abused another man or woman, or every woman who has molested a boy or girl is a pedophile. When adults molest and abuse kids in the family, the cycle will continue until we educate our kids and make sexuality a comfortable subject to talk about.

Children who have been abused by a relative need the unconditional love and support of their families. A therapist who specializes in sexual abuse and assault can help a lot. But it may not be safe for the child to have certain members of the family in their support system, if they don't believe the child or side with the abuser. Most importantly, the child has to hear that it is not her or his fault! I know adults who are still wrestling with guilt and shame from their childhood. A spiritual component to healing for any family would not hurt as long as it is kept within the context of their values and belief system. This could help keep the child from developing a victim identity. I remember reading a study or report that said girls who are sexually abused are more likely to become prostitutes than girls who aren't. There are a lot of studies out there on the abuse histories of prostitutes.

If I had kids and they told me they were being sexually abused by anyone in the family, I'd let them know I believe them first and foremost. The second thing I would do is make sure my child is safe. Guaranteeing that safety would consist of calling the authorities and pressing charges. If the abuser was a peer to my child, I would involve the authorities to simply ensure that both families are involved in a cooperative effort to get therapeutic counseling. I would assume that a young child or teenager sexually molesting my child has also been abused. If the abuser is an adult, I would prosecute and ask the court to make sure my family member receives counseling and participates in a program to educate communities and family members on sexual abuse within families. These are the action steps I would take regardless of who the family member is—immediate or extended, male or female.

I would be hurt and probably blame myself more than the average parent because this is my field. I'd think things like, *"You are educated about the signs of abuse. You are the one person who should've been able to prevent something like this from happening to your own child.*" In order to keep myself from taking on the guilt and shame of someone else's actions, I'd join a support group for parents of children who have been sexually abused and possibly see a therapist individually. Depending on my child's age, I'd put them in an empowering support group that uses the arts for healing. But this would only be done if my child was comfortable and ready. They would not be forced to do anything they did not want to, including testifying. As long as my kids know they are loved unconditionally and that the sexual abusive act of another family member does not define or limit them in anyway, I know I have done the best I can do.

Why do you think African American families don't discuss or disclose child sexual abuse when it happens within their family?

How do you think an African American child who has been victimized within their family is affected when no one acknowledges or deals with what happened?

In my opinion, Black people care about what others think of them too much. I was taught to *"keep family business in the family."* I think many families, regardless of race, are ingrained with this same message. I've seen this carried out to the detriment of people who have suffered in silence. Black people need to raise their consciousness and realize nobody has the power to label us. Those are just words. You can empower yourself.

Look at our history. Black men had to stand by and watch their wives, sisters, mothers and daughters be raped by white men but couldn't do anything about it. Now we've gotten to a point where we are committing this crime against each other and pointing the finger and blaming someone else. Sibling abuse or incestuous abuse between relatives close in age seems to be played down by adults...

Historically, white people were threatened by our sexuality, especially Black women. They tried to confine us and actually did— Sarah Bartmann, aka the Hottentot Venus*, being one of the earlier cases. Then they brought us their religion in an effort to save us from "sin." But that still didn't stop white priests from raping and molesting little Black boys in Africa. Read Patrice Malidoma's, *Of Water and the Spirit*. Christianity, in the way it was presented and applied, was not the answer. This is obvious today with the number of people coming forward about being sexually abused and molested by reverends and priests—it's not just Catholics!

---

* Saartjie Bartmann, commonly known as Sarah or the Hottentot Venus, was a South African Khoikhoi woman born in the late 18th century. She was caged and exhibited throughout Europe to highlight the large size of her buttocks and labia. Upon her death at the early age of 25, her organs were put on display in a Paris museum until 1974. With the help of Nelson Mandela and other advocates her remains were finally returned to her birth place in 2002.

Knowing what happened to Black women and girls historically, I assumed Black men would rally around women and protect them from harm whenever it was in their capability to do so. Some men do this, and I love and cherish them. They are speaking up. Unfortunately, there still exists an ingrained belief as strong as institutionalized racism that women and girls are the sexual property of men. African American communities and families of color are not excluded from this socialization. When incestuous abuse within the family actually comes out where a man has abused a girl, instead of dealing with it, some Black women protect the man. If the abuser is the woman's partner, she might not do anything. If the abuser is someone in the extended family, whispers and phone calls behind closed doors may start. *"Keep the kids away from Cousin Ted. You no he ain't right in the head."* But no one directly confronts Cousin Ted and brings it out in the open—let alone report the crime he has committed. Believe me, he will strike again.

A few years ago, I knew a woman from Sierra Leone. I asked her about incest and if it occurred in her country. She told me it was very rare. According to her, if it did occur the male perpetrator and abused female would have to walk throughout the entire village for the day, naked. Afterwards, she said, the man and girl were taken to a river to be spiritually cleansed. I shared this story with a white co-worker who was actually interested in adopting Black children. She liked the concept because, in her opinion, at least it's out in the open. No one in the village points the finger and laughs at these people. Everyone knows. There is a spiritual cleansing ceremony and they are accepted back into society.

I asked a Black woman what she thought of this African concept. She's a survivor of incest. She had a big problem with it. She ranted and raved about how it wasn't right and the child was made to feel ashamed. But this woman does not know if the African child was ashamed or not. She based her opinion off American culture. My first reaction was the same as my friend. I thought, *"That's not right! The man should be made to walk around naked and locked up!"* But then I considered a possibility that the African brothers and sisters in that village of Sierra Leone where my friend grew up, were not trying to humiliate or shame anybody. They were trying to purge themselves.

I don't have all the answers as to how we as Black people in this country should deal with abuse. But I like the African concept of not hiding from it at the very least. I like the idea that the entire village knows and comes together to cleanse the perpetrator and the innocent child. My friend was 30 years old when she told me this story. She had only been in the U.S. for a couple years and only remembered seeing this happen one time in her life. I wish I could say that when I had turned 30, I only knew of one person who had been sexually abused by someone in his/her family.

Conclusion

We will keep re-infecting each other and completely destroy the most valuable, precious part of American society, our children, unless we take action to accept sexuality as something sacred. We are worthy of *respect*. If any of us believe we come from a divine source of love that wants us to have a joyful life of peace, free from pain, we must do whatever is necessary to end the needless suffering we inflict upon each other. In spite of the distress many people live with daily, there are still those who believe we live in a society that is sexually free and liberated. Progress has been made, but we still have a long way to go.

Now that you have read the Peterson family's story, I am sure you identified with some of their opinions and beliefs. I commend and respect them for having the courage to say in private what many people will not say publicly to avoid being deemed "politically incorrect" or because of the fear of being judged by others.

Think of your own belief system and examine how you were conditioned to be the person you are. Did past messages and teachings of sexuality make you feel secure or vulnerable? Consider exploring the values, beliefs and experiences within your sexuality. Are they a reflection of who you are or of who someone else wants you to be? Was there someone in your family who behaved in a sexual way that does not sit well with you in the pit of your stomach? What secrets exist within your own family that people know but do not speak about? If it is too frightening to ask these questions of yourself at this time, re-read the Peterson family's testimonies. After you have read their stories again, I ask you to be daring in your own life.

Take action and accept sexuality as sacred by empowering yourself. Analyze your past and present social conditioning about sexuality with a critical eye and shed any messages that do not serve or reflect the essence of you. Explore your family upbringing and discard any teachings or verbal programming that has weakened your spirit. Any thought, word or behavior which did not or does not support a positive image of yourself is harmful to you. Do not let these messages infect the next generation of people in your family or community. Education is powerful. The next generation can learn from our experiences only if we share them—no matter how painful some of them are.

My hope for the Peterson family is that they will reflect on their lives, begin to talk openly and empower the next generation of children within their family with accurate information about sexuality. Open communication and education are necessary steps in beginning to decrease the numbers of children and teenagers being sexually abused within our families. True power comes from knowing, without hesitation, that you have the right to speak up when someone violates you. Now is the time to shed the history of our sexual oppression. We do not need to remain quiet nor does it serve us to keep things *hush-hush* anymore.

If we have the Word let us

say it.

If we have the Word let us

be it.

If we have the Word let us

DO.

- Mari Evans, Nightstar: 1973-1978

Resources

Recommended Books

Angelou, M. (1983). *I Know Why the Caged Bird Sings*. New York: Bantam Books.

Bryant, S. P. (2005). *Hung: A Meditation on the Measure of Black Men in America*. New York: Harlem Moon, Broadway Books.

Goldenflame, J. (2005). *Overcoming Sexual Terrorism: How to Protect Your Children from Sexual Predators*. Lincoln, Nebraska: iUniverse Inc.

Hamilton, B. S. (1997). *The Hidden Legacy: Uncovering, Confronting and Healing Three Generations of Incest*. Fort Bragg, California: Cypress House.

Leary, J. D. (2005). *Post Traumatic Slave Syndrome: America's Legacy of Enduring Injury and Healing*. Milwaukie, Oregon: Uptone Press.

Preble, J. M., and Groth, A. N. (2002). *Male Victims of Same-Sex Abuse: Addressing Their Sexual Response*. Baltimore, MD: Sidran Press.

Robinson, L. S. (2002). *I Will Survive: The African-American Guide to Healing from Sexual Assault and Abuse*. New York: Seal Press.

Rose, T. (2004). *Longing to Tell: Black Women Talk about Sexuality and Intimacy*. New York: Picador.

Russell, D. E. H. (1999). *The Secret Trauma: Incest in the Lives of Girls and Women*. New York: Basic Books.

Sapphire. (1997). *Push*. New York: Vintage Contemporaries, Vintage Books.

Stone, R. (2005). *No Secrets No Lies: How Black Families Can Heal From Sexual Abuse*. New York: Broadway Books.

Walker, A. (1985). *The Color Purple*. New York: Pocket Books.

Wyatt, G. E. (1997). *Stolen Women: Reclaiming Our Sexuality, Taking Back Our Lives*. New York: John Wiley & Sons, Inc.

Recommended Films & Documentaries

Antwone Fisher – released in 2002

This true story directed by Denzel Washington is based on Antwone's Fisher's life. It shows how he overcame growing up in an abusive foster family to eventually find his biological family and release troubling experiences from his past.

Hip Hop: Beyond Beats and Rhymes – released in 2006
www.bhurt.com

Filmmaker and gender violence prevention educator Byron Hurt directed and co-produced this ground breaking documentary that focuses on masculinity, sexism, misogyny and homophobia in hip hop culture and music.

NO! The Rape Documentary – released in 2006
www.notherapedocumentary.org

Filmmaker Aishah Shahida Simmons produced, wrote and directed this award-winning documentary. This film examines rape and sexual violence in the African American community through interviews with female survivors, scholars and community leaders.

Woman Thou Art Loosed – released in 2005

Based on a novel by Bishop T. D. Jakes, this story shows a young woman in prison recalling painful memories from her past. After surviving being raped by her mother's boyfriend, lead character Michelle, played by Kimberly Elise, turns to a life of drugs and prostitution. Bishop T. D. Jakes portrays himself in the film and helps Michelle process the mistakes she made in her life in an effort to heal from her painful past.

Advocacy & Research

A Call to Men
Phone: 917-922-6738
www.acalltomen.com

A Call To Men, is a leading national men's organization addressing men's violence against women and the eradication of sexism. The organization helps mobilize communities in order to raise awareness and get men involved in ending violence against women. Through seminars, workshops and other educational vehicles, A Call To Men challenges men to reconsider their long held beliefs about women in an effort to create a more just society.

Male Survivor
www.malesurvivor.org

Male Survivor is an organization committed to preventing, healing and eliminating all forms of sexual victimization of boys and men through treatment, research, education, advocacy and activism. The organization puts on national conferences and has extensive resources on their website for male survivors, professionals and concerned citizens.

Rape, Abuse and Incest National Network (RAINN)
National Sexual Assault Hotline: 1-800-656-HOPE
www.rainn.org

The Rape, Abuse & Incest National Network is the nation's largest anti-sexual assault organization. RAINN operates the National Sexual Assault Hotline and carries out programs to prevent sexual assault, provide resources for victims and ensure that rapists are brought to justice. Local rape crisis centers can be found on RAINN's website.

Sexuality Information and Education Council (SIECUS)
www.siecus.org

SIECUS, the Sexuality Information and Education Council of the United States, has served as the national voice for sexuality education, sexual health and sexual rights for over 40 years. SIECUS affirms that sexuality is a fundamental part of being human, one that is worthy of dignity and respect. They advocate for the right of all people to access accurate information and comprehensive education about sexuality and sexual health services. SIECUS works to create a world that ensures social justice and sexual rights.

Jim Hopper, PhD
www.jimhopper.com

Dr. Jim Hopper is a researcher and instructor in psychology at Harvard Medical School. His website contains sections offering a multitude of relevant, up-to-date information and research on child sexual abuse and specifically, the sexual abuse of males.

References

1. Douglas, E. M., Finkelhor, D. (2005, May). *Child Sexual Abuse Fact Sheet*. Retrieved April 18, 2007 from University of New Hampshire, Crimes Against Children Research Center website: http://www.unh.edu/ccrc/factsheet/index.html.

2. Abney, V. D., Priest, R. (1995). African Americans and Sexual Child Abuse. In L. Fontes (Ed.) *Sexual Abuse in Nine North American Cultures: Treatment and Prevention*, (p. 19), Thousand Oaks: Sage Publications.

3. Gaffney, D.A. (2003). Sexuality and Sexual Behaviors in Adolescence. In Gaffney, D. A., Roye, C. (Eds.). *Adolescent Sexual Development and Sexuality – Assessment and Interventions*, (p. 7–2), Kingston, New Jersey: Civic Research Center.

4. Roye, C. F. (2003). Sexual Development in the Male and Female. In Gaffney, D. A., Roye, C. (Eds.) *Adolescent Sexual Development and Sexuality: Assessment and Interventions*, (p. 1–1), Kingston, New Jersey: Civic Research Institute.

5. Wyatt, G. E. (1997). *Stolen Women: Reclaiming Our Sexuality, Taking Back Our Lives*, (p. 225), New York: John Wiley & Sons, Inc.

6. Authorized King James Version. (1979). *The Holy Bible*. Nashville: Holman Bible Publishers.

7. Mayo Foundation for Medical Education and Research. (2007, April). *Sex Education: Talking to Toddlers and Preschoolers About Sex.* Retrieved April 18, 2007 from: http://www.mayoclinic.com/health/sex-education/HQ00547.

8. Mayo Foundation for Medical Education and Research. (2005). *Sex Education: Start Discussions Early.* Retrieved December 19, 2006 from: http://www.mayoclinic.com/health/parenting/CC00050.

9. Henry J. Kaiser Family Foundation. (1998). *National Survey of Teens: Teens Talk About Dating, Intimacy, and Their Sexual Experiences.* Retrieved April 25, 2007 from: http://www.kff.org/youthhivstds/1373-datingrep.cfm.

10. Center for Disease Control and Prevention. (2000). Youth Risk Behavior Surveillance – United States, 1999. *Morbidity and Mortality Weekly Report, 49(SS–5).*

11. Moshner, W. D., Chandra, A., Jones, J. (2005). Sexual Behavior and Selected Health Measures: Men and Women 15-44 Years of Age, United States, 2002. *Advance Data from Vital and Health Statistics, 362.* Retrieved April 25, 2007 from National Center for Health Statistics website: http://www.cdc.gov/nchs/products/pubs/pubd/ad/361-370/ad362.htm.

12. Gaffney, D.A. (2003). Sexuality and Sexual Behaviors in Adolescence. In Gaffney, D. A., Roye, C. (Eds.). *Adolescent Sexual Development and Sexuality – Assessment and Interventions,* (p. 7–5), Kingston, New Jersey: Civic Research Center.

13. Synder, H. N. (2000, July). *Sexual Assault of Young Children as Reported to Law Enforcement: Victim, Incident, and Offender Characteristics.* Retrieved January 11, 2007 from U.S. Department of Justice, Bureau of Justice Statistics website: http://www.ojp.usdoj.gov/bjs/abstract/saycrle.htm.

14. Miller, P. (2006, June, 25). Complaints of Sexual Abuse by Nuns Begin to Emerge. *Minneapolis Star Tribune,* Retrieved April 28, 2007 from The Survivors Network of Those Abused by Priest website: http://www.snapnetwork.org/female_victims/complaints_abuse_by_nuns.htm.

15. Longo, R. E., (2000, August). *Myths and Facts About Sex Offenders.* Retrieved January 11, 2007 from Office of Justice Programs, U.S. Department of Justice, Center for Sex Offender Management website: http://www.csom.org/pubs/mythsfacts.html.

16. Synder, H. N. (2000, July). *Sexual Assault of Young Children as Reported to Law Enforcement: Victim, Incident, and Offender Characteristics.* Retrieved January 11, 2007 from U.S. Department of Justice, Bureau of Justice Statistics website: http://www.ojp.usdoj.gov/bjs/abstract/saycrle.htm.

17. Russell, D. E. H. (1999). *The Secret Trauma: Incest in the Lives of Girls and Women, (revised edition),* (p. 85), New York: Basic Books.

18. Hopper, J. (revised 2007, March). *Sexual Abuse of Males: Prevalence, Possible Lasting Effects, & Resources.* Retrieved April 18, 2007 from: http://www.jimhopper.com/male-ab/.

19. Preble, J. M., Groth, A. N. (2002). *Male Victims of Same-Sex Abuse: Addressing Their Sexual Response,* (p. 7), Baltimore, Maryland: Sidran Press.

20. Russell, D. E. H. (1999). *The Secret Trauma: Incest in the Lives of Girls and Women*, *(revised edition)*, (p. 39), New York: Basic Books.

21. American Psychiatric Association. (2000). *Diagnostic and Statistical Manual of Mental Disorders*, (4th *edition, text revision*). Washington DC.

22. Preble, J. M., and Groth, A. N. (2002). *Male Victims of Same-Sex Abuse: Addressing Their Sexual Response*, (pp. 42–44), Baltimore, Maryland: Sidran Press.

23. Preble, J.M. and Groth, A. N. p. 46.

24. Mullen, P. E., Fleming, J. (1998). Long-term effects of child sexual abuse. *Issues in Child Abuse Prevention, 9.* Retrieved March 14, 2007 from Australian Institute of Family Studies, National Child Protection Clearing House website: http://www.aifs.gov.au/nch/issues9.html.

25. Lowe, T., Pavkov, T. W., Casanova, G. M., Wetchler, J. L. (2005). Do ethnic cultures differ in their definitions of child sexual abuse? *The American Journal of Family Therapy.* 33, 147–166.

26. Leary, J. D. (2005). *Post Traumatic Slave Syndrome: America's Legacy of Enduring Injury and Healing*, (p.123), Milwaukie, Oregon: Uptone Press.

27. Rape, Abuse and Incest National Network (RAINN). Retrieved November 30, 2006 from: http://www.rainn.org/statistics/victims-of-sexual-assault.html.

About the Author

DeShannon Bowens is a therapist, staff development trainer and founder of ILERA Counseling and Education Services. She founded ILERA to educate and raise awareness about cultural factors influencing sexuality and help survivors and their families heal from the effects of sexual abuse. Ms. Bowens has a bachelor's degree in psychology from the University of Missouri–St. Louis, as well as a master's degree in counseling from Pace University in Pleasantville, New York. Her professional experience includes a solid foundation in mental health research and counseling. In an effort to take her message to the airwaves, Ms. Bowens has appeared on WBAI 99.5 FM Peace and Justice Radio in New York City as a producer and talk radio host for segments of the semi-annual *Hip Hop Takeover* marathon. Her shows focused on the intersection of hip hop music and sexuality. For more information about DeShannon Bowens and her organization's services, please feel free to contact her through her website at www.ilera.com.